To Sid

Hope this is useful.

A Pain In The **R**s

Where Is The **R**espect, **R**eward And **R**ecognition I Deserve?

A Pain In The Rs

Where Is The **R**espect, **R**eward And **R**ecognition I Deserve?

By

John Ricades

Revised March 2014

A Pain In The **R**s

Where Is The **R**espect, **R**eward And **R**ecognition I Deserve?

By

John Ricades

ISBN: 978-0-9926729-0-4

Printed by: BookPrintingUK.com

Bonacia Ltd, Remus House, Coltsfoot Drive

Peterborough, Cambridgeshire PE2 9BF

This book is self-published by J^2R^2R.

First Edition 2013

NOTE: The information contained within this book is correct at time of being published and liable to change.

Foreword

"A Pain In The Rs – Where Is The Respect, Reward And Recognition I Deserve" is a book about experiencing a lack of respect, reward and recognition by John, a gifted, brain damaged individual who was subjected to years of oppression, emotional abuse and had his natural progress suppressed by bureaucrats in authority who got him labelled inappropriately. The journey this book takes you along goes in all directions and so you will need to get stuck in to realise where you are going. Just like going north to get onto a motorway to head much further south, the direction at the start is nothing like further along. When you get to the destination you will see it is all for the better; but it didn't come without a long battle with bureaucratic control freaks.

John, who like many under-rated victims has experienced a life of extremes with little or no support when he needed it the most; but still managed to succeed in his own self-taught way albeit not via the usual channels and consequently a lot of talent has gone to waste as well as used in defence and destruction against persistent oppression exercised by officials in positions of authority.

People in authority prefer members of the public to be led and follow like sheep being told what to do; but they don't like individuals who think and reason for themselves and stand up to anything which they see as "inappropriate". This could explain why John was subjected to so much emotional abuse.

Having the ability to understand some maths worthy of A-level standard in junior school (1972) without any private tuition or mentoring and using his imagination to come up with new ideas John was seen as an ideal child, but at the time he was already seeing a child psychiatrist as he had many problems being too advanced for his age, especially with some officials in authority trying to restrict his natural progress which John didn't like and felt imprisoned. This made John very irritable against being restricted and so he wasn't going to cooperate when he was treated in the wrong for being different, and wasn't going to let their mental limitations restrict his progress.

Less than a year later in 1973 when he started having temporal lobe epilepsy he was put on a cocktail of drugs which affected his behaviour and with all the extra restrictions and pressure he was being put under combined with the trauma and not being listened to but treated as if he was to blame for everything, it got too much for him and he started to use violence and destruction to defend himself as things were becoming unbearable. He ended up being sectioned and admitted into adults' psychiatric hospital for five months at the age of twelve where he was regularly sedated with Valium and locked up in a cell; and in doing so got abused by cruel nurses.

Over the years John has demonstrated some amazing brain power as well as using mind over matter to overcome many hurdles and obstacles put in his way by oppressors in authority, and with determination after many years of trying and not giving up managed to get away from the stranglehold of the authorities. He has also been something of a challenge for many in authority since if things weren't right John would not take it peacefully and many people were afraid of John when he got worked up.

John's experiences suggests there are too many useless currants in positions of authority with mentalities like cowards from The Weakest Link looking for excuses to undermine individuals who are stronger so that as cowards they can stay on top. John's handicap was used to undermine his intelligence and his intelligence was used to undermine his care needs – so John was living in a "black hole" for twenty years (1973 to 1993) being treated as an outcast.

During this time John didn't get any support for his care needs or any opportunity or recognition for his potential. This was making him act very much out of character and he wasn't himself for most of the time. This doesn't mean to say that John had difficulties with everyone – the problems lay with a minority who always wanted to be put first and in control; whereas people who treated John the same as how they expected to be treated John got on well with. So this is a reflection of what the minority obsessed with control can cause.

In spite of all these "artificial barriers" and having regular seizures John wasn't going to be beaten by the illness or being labelled by the authorities. He always got a warning when a seizure was about to happen so could prepare for it.

John had significant strengths before he was a teenager whom he was too much for many in authority to handle, especially when it was down to inappropriate treatment and unfairness. As a result, John had a hatred of people in positions of authority that abused their authority and spoke to him in the wrong tone of voice to undermine him, and consequently if they didn't leave him alone John lashed out at various people in authority for treating him "inappropriately". John could read between the lines at what was going on – the body language, tone of voice and words used against him were inappropriate and nothing more than a cover-up of failure within the authorities.

Since John wasn't getting any support, he had to teach himself discipline and using his analytical skills he could tell that they weren't putting his needs first but appeared to be using him as a stepping stone for their progress, so he would look at ways of progressing in parallel with the authorities which wasn't popular as John was always acting like an escapee. If he worked in series they would have been the weakest link in his chain and weakened his development.

John's story explains how inappropriate treatment by oppressors in authority changed him from once being someone described as "**A very capable boy who has been most cooperative during the year - he has**

good all round ability but is particularly good in maths at which he could go a long way" into one of the most disruptive and destructive of people who for many years was bottom of the class and caused more unrest within society than many without getting into trouble because it was all a backlash at how he had been treated.

It also shows how these oppressors abuse their powers and use vulnerable people to tread on and abuse to feel better in themselves; but as John is a survivor and wise to what went on he is now able to reveal what these control freaks would rather keep suppressed. That is the main objective of this book as what he went through wants to be forgotten by the authorities.

All this happened between 1973 and 1993 while John was living in the Bridgend area of South Wales, which in 2008 became globally known as **The Suicide Capital of the UK**. During these twenty years of oppression he didn't receive a single penny in disability benefits for his care needs, and in spite of his intelligence he was treated as subnormal. In 1993 John relocated to Lancashire and went into business, and in 1996 underwent brain surgery and was cured of epilepsy.

John has moved on and proven that the authorities were restraining his progress for if he was what they had labelled him as he wouldn't be where he is now; so obviously officials in the various authorities in South Wales were out to restrict his progress which held him back; but the authorities tried to make it look like John's own weakness, not their enforced restrictions on him. As John wasn't given the chance to make the most of his potential and this was restricted by people in high positions of authority who weren't particularly talented but nothing more than spoon-fed bureaucrats, exercising false one-upmanship. He doesn't respect authority and won't recognise those at the top as the best since if many were like those who treated him inappropriately, most at the top would be cheats and cowards looking for opportunity to bully those who are more capable.

People who can rise to high positions naturally are genuine; whereas those who cheat and suppress the progress of others to make themselves look better are the ones who are obsessed with coming out on top at all costs and wouldn't be worthy of their positions in the fair world. They are the types who abuse others for progress and there are many victims of this type of abuse – especially with gifted individuals from poor or disadvantaged backgrounds. John will only respect people for their capabilities who are genuine and have shown potential worthy of their position and not had an easy ride or everything handed to them on a plate, since too many who have had it easy have exercised false one-upmanship and been too cocky.

If you met John on a good day, you wouldn't think he has been through what he has since this is when this is his true character; but it only takes someone to be a bit domineering, manipulative, to invert the truth against him, speak to him in the wrong tone of voice or criticise him for not doing what they want and his character can change into someone quite nasty. This is a reflection of how John had to go about defending himself when he went through his years of development as peaceful defence didn't work.

Acknowledgements

The following individuals I must show some level of thanks to for helping me through hard times, directly or indirectly, having caught my imagination recognising what potential there is out there, and made life more interesting. It is quite the opposite of being isolated when some of our earlier adventures which happened before the internet was available and are now well talked about. Some of the places I went are mentioned in a bit more detail later on. I didn't know up front what was behind them and probably wouldn't have without the internet.

Donald Richard
My father (1933 to 1964) was a very well-liked man who was brought up in the Kenfig Hill area, but sadly died young (aged 30 in 1964) from injury and infection. His legacy has left me with something to be proud of and although I can be a Jekyll and Hyde my natural character is similar when things are right.

Jane
My mother has had to endure a lot of upset over the years but she has stood behind me and got me through the many hurdles and wars with life. Although I haven't got a lot to show I am sure she is proud of me just like I am of her. She hasn't had much in the way of quality in her life helping me cope with the problems which shouldn't have happened in the first place.

Herbert Martin
Herbert knew my father from early days and remembered him as his best friend who would always do what he could and was always calm. In 2013 Herbert wanted to remember my father by having a gravestone put on his grave in St James' Church as it was only a basic grave and it has now been done – see later.

Christopher Kelly
A friend from early infants' days who I knew until about 1969 then didn't see until after 2000. Christopher meant a lot in my very early days and remembers me challenging the teachers and answering them back when I was in my first year of infants' school at only five years of age.

Peter James Wood
A good friend I got to know at St Bede's School who was originally from the

Chichester area. I muddled Chichester up with Christchurch and thought it was near Bournemouth. I got to know an uncle of his in the Brocton area of Cannock Chase who used to be a policeman.

JJ Williams

My mother once worked for the rugby player JJ Williams at his business on Village Farm Industrial Estate. He was already well known and it was a pleasure to meet him.

Kevin Loye

A long-term friend I first met at school in Port Talbot back in 1970. Even today we keep in touch and share memories over the years. The town has connections with actors Antony Hopkins, Richard Burton and Michael Sheen which regularly gets mentioned with the town as well as the pollution and the steel works. I know the town as "**P**ollution **O**f **R**eal **T**hreat **T**o **A**ll **L**iving **B**eings **O**ut **T**here". We reminisce on our school days sharing the good times with the bad times.

Michael Loye, Martin Rock, Terrance Thomas & Others

To these and all friends from school days who supported me in various ways.

All Teachers At Corneli Junior School

This was probably the best of my school days before all the problems started with epilepsy. In 1972 it was the last time I got the recognition I deserved. Mr Hare, Mr Jones, Mr Williams, Mr Walton, Mr Leyshon, Mr Hughes, Mrs Richards, and not to forget the secretary Mrs Gentry. The report I got is the last true reflection of my potential which I treasure and have included it in this book.

Maldwyn

Maldwyn was a milkman for Bridgend Creameries who I used to help collect payments for after junior school on a Friday afternoon. I was only about eleven years old and one day I was daydreaming when collecting some money from a customer on Ffordd-yr-Eglwys by Ael-y-Bryn when the customer (a ragbag of a woman) accused me of being rude just because when she answered I was thinking of something else. She shouted at me and towards Maldwyn of which I ran off in tears and never saw Maldwyn again. I couldn't face up to being blamed for doing nothing wrong so sorry Maldwyn, you meant a lot to me but that old ragbag upset me beyond acceptance.

Jeff Kent

Jeff was a hairdresser who had his business in premises at the top of Pisgah Street in Kenfig Hill close to what was the old railway line which separated Bridge Street from Pisgah Street. Jeff was a gentleman and so positive and respectful. He was one of the few people who would see the best in people. As a result he never saw the bad side of me – and that is how I preferred to be seen. He always brought the best out in me and spoke the best of me.

Rae John

Rae owned a bookshop in Porthcawl called The Library and it was where I would order the books I wanted. She was only the owner but she helped me get what I wanted. I have met her and reminded her of her services and how much she meant to me when I was in school.

All Artists Who Supplied Music

Popular music through the 1960s and the early to mid-1970s (including ones which were popular from earlier years) I used to listen to a lot. It was my main form of relaxation as well as got many frustrations out of me. Even today many of the tracks which were around then still give me a boost. Music has meant a lot in relaxation to me as I have a good ear for music.

Lloyd Williams

Lloyd was a short-term friend who I met while out on cycling in 1978. He was from Maesteg with his mother Shelia a nurse and his father Clive a coach driver. I haven't seen him since 1980.

Brandon Thomas Davies

Brandon was a short-tern friend who I met at Tycoch College in Swansea and was from the Portmead area of Swansea. We worked together as students and were known as The Dynamic Duo. I haven't seen him since 1980 either.

Lynda Shuker

A friend I met at Tycoch College in Swansea who lived just off Plunch Lane in Mumbles, just down the road from where Catherine Zeta-Jones (CZJ) and Michel Douglas live. Lynda went to Dumbarton House School in Swansea which is where CZJ went. I got to know the Limeslade and Bracelet Bay area of Mumbles not knowing the fame destined for this part of Swansea Bay. I also got to know the Uplands area of Swansea as this is where I used to get all my books (Uplands Bookshop) and the college was nearby. I also ventured around Cwmdonkin Park; this is the area where Dylan Thomas was brought up (not knowing this at the time), as well as other parts of Swansea including Cwmbwrla, Brynhyfryd, Portmead, Penlan, Blaen-y-Maes, Port Tennant and Morriston.

Howard Marks

Howard Marks was a very intelligent man, slightly older than me from Kenfig Hill, who went to Oxford University and became a drugs baron. We heard a lot about him locally and eventually he became known as Mr Nice and did a book on his accomplishments. He shed some light on extremes within society even though I don't like the thought of misuse of drugs.

Doreen Roberts

Doreen, a colleague who worked with me when I had epilepsy, has been kept up-to-date of my progress and passed information on to other colleagues.

Mr Eldridge

The surgeon who operated on my brain at The Walton Centre in Liverpool in 1996 which was a success and this has made a big difference to my overall quality of life. I thank all his team as well.

Anne Nolan

Quite by chance after settling down in the Blackpool area and singing St Cuthbert's Church choir on Lytham Road, I came across Anne from The Nolan Sisters who I wasn't aware of who she was at first. We got to know each other through the choir and I was complimented for my singing.

Paul Wilkins

A friend I met in 1999, also experienced medical problems like I did, but in a different way. He has had more problems internally and struggles with life; but I am someone who he finds very understanding and I help him where possible as he writes plenty of poems which have a positive charm about them.

Mr Sagar

The surgeon who operated and removed my colon at Leeds General Infirmary to take away the pain I was in. this too has made life more comfortable. I thank all his team as well.

Gerry Wakefield

A patient from Leeds who used to be a coach driver was in Leeds General Infirmary when I underwent treatment who was interested in aerospace and we became friends. We have been around various places in the UK together exploring.

Joan Foster

Joan was an auntie on my mother's side that supported me until I had conflict with her son. This cousin was rather stubborn and wouldn't listen. His beliefs he treated as fact and he would ridicule the truth. This became a barrier between us and broke the family up because he was blaming me for things which weren't true and I wouldn't accept his domination. They won't forgive me for my defence against untrue beliefs and it is a shame as Joan meant a lot to me.

Sylvia Fosberry

A prominent person within Lions Clubs International who has always been supportive and never been negative towards me, she has offered support and been behind my objectives.

Craig Eckersley

A friend who I have known since 2006 and we go exploring not just in the UK but also abroad as well. He contributes a lot to the Royal Aeronautical Society and I have visited various aerospace establishments and museums at home and abroad with him and groups he organises.

Philip Scott

A hotel proprietor from Blackpool involved with Speakers and has been very supportive in many ways.

Philip Ford

A former pupil of Lingfield Hospital School who has helped me piece together some of my times at the school and remember some of the other pupils too. I didn't know of him until 2007 at a reunion and we have stayed in touch since.

Martin Hossack

Once owner of the domain dwpcorruption.co.uk who I came across and found out more of what really goes on within government departments and the collusion between solicitors and the public services to present many of us especially the vulnerable who cannot fight for themselves from getting justice and the treatment they deserve. Martin certainly made me aware of how vast the many problems within society are.

Clive Bradley
Clive was a member of staff at Lingfield Hospital School and he was one of the few I could talk to and would listen to me. I managed to trace him down around 2008 and he certainly remembered me for my difference in character and how determined I was to move on with life. We regularly meet up and share ideas and it is nice to have a good connection with a troublesome period in my life.

Teresa Cooper
Author of the book ***Trust No One*** which is a reflection of the abuse she suffered at the hands of the authorities and at an establishment run by The Church of England. She and I are friends and we are trying to make the public more aware of what forms of child abuse goes on and how widespread it is as well as how reluctant the institutions and governments are to admit their role in letting this abuse take place.

ASSIST – Trauma Support, Rugby, Warwickshire
ASSIST helped me with support and advice, and it was they who identified the type of PTSD I have as Developmental Trauma Disorder.

Ken Dodd
I have admired Ken for years and thought that Knotty Ash was a make-believe place until I came across it by chance. I have had connections indirectly with Ken through publishing poems written by Paul about Ken and he knows Pat Modley who is now my lover. One song I have liked for many years is **Think Of Me** which Pat likes and I have sang it to her on many occasions.

Pat Modley
Originally from Brighton Pat, my lover now, was a Tiller Girl in her younger days and has performed on stage at various theatres in London, Blackpool and Brighton. I came across Pat while taking part in various speakers' events connected with The Association of Speakers' Clubs and now we have a relationship. Pat is the daughter-in-law of comedian Albert Modley who was originally from Ilkley in West Yorkshire and established himself in the Lancashire seaside town of Morecambe. I know Ilkley as I have relatives in nearby Menston. For many years Pat lived in Haywards Heath

in West Sussex and this was one of the areas I explored when I ran away from the special school I was in back in 1974. Pat has appeared on stage and TV with Morecambe and Wise, Bruce Forsyth and knows Ken Dodd. Pat has had close connections with other stars too. Pat also once ran the family business Modley's in Morecambe which was a restaurant and had several rooms for accommodation of which some stars including Bruce Forsyth and Ken Dodd have dined and stayed at. It is a pity I hadn't met Pat earlier on. When it comes to music, four songs we regularly enjoy singing together: **Annie's Song; All I Have To Do Is Dream; Think Of Me**; and **Me and Mrs Jones**.

Michael Sheen

It was a great experience to take part in The Passion around the streets of Port Talbot in 2011.

Lorraine Ireland

A hypnotist from Kinver in Staffordshire who has helped me put my mind to rest over much of the trauma I went through. I don't know she trains the mind but it works somehow.

Marion Middleditch

A friend of Pat, who helped me become more relaxed and confident in my speaking and performing in public. It has helped me feel more relaxed generally and she could see I was afraid of performing to the full. She even suggested that during earlier days I had been singled out and made a fool of because I had a fear of performing to the full. She has helped me here.

Mike Hall

Mike who is a recognised actor and singer in Blackpool has taught me how to use my voice more. I have had singing lessons with him for a while now and taken part in concerts in various choruses. He understands the problems within society where some expect too much for little talent and others with greater potential are ignored.

Brian Prescott

Brian ran a course for Cognitive Behaviour Therapy in nearby Cleveleys which has helped me to be more relaxed. The individuals I came across were different to the stereotypical image perceived by many.

Those I Have Missed Out

There are many other individuals I come across who are worthy of making me value life. It could be with a complete stranger as I travel about the UK or abroad and I wish that there were more individuals like them. There are thousands of you but I cannot pinpoint you all.

The Disruptive Streak

The disruptive streak I have has saved me from having my life ruined by control freaks in positions of authority. I became too much for many and this streak has helped me move on although rather destructively.

Determination

I am not going to give up as I believe something is watching over me and as a survivor I have a duty to expose what went on and be myself to the full without fear of persecution by those who cannot accept me for what I am. Nature and the truth appear to be on my side as a gift from Mother Nature is far stronger than anything handed to some on a plate. The gravity exercised by those with power and control linked to status and wealth expecting others to revolve around them like planets is nowhere near the strength of gravity which Mother Nature has.

Finally

Power In The Hands Of The Weak section is a collection of different scenarios and circumstances where deliberate wrongdoing has been committed for progress and so is an analysis of possibilities from different perspectives. It may be a bit boring for some, but could uproot some thoughts for others. They aren't to be applied to everyone but where applicable. It is like BMW drivers – many are decent drivers, but you have a handful of privileged attention-seeking idiots trying to make out they are better showing off and thus giving the impression all BMW drivers are bad. This luxury of putting power in the hands of the weak is where many problems within society originate. It is always down to smaller people standing on higher platforms trying to look bigger because they don't like the truth being seen as smaller – in other words they cannot accept the truth of their relative inferiority. It is always decent, talented, more capable people who are targeted by these weaklings – a bit like how cowards on The Weakest Link gang up against the strongest to use the power of the vote and ignore the facts to make the strongest look the weakest. Anyone who comes out on top like this is automatically seen as a coward on top.

Index

Power In The Hands Of The Weak 125

Outline Of Life

On April 1st 1996 I underwent brain surgery at The Walton Centre in Liverpool and this has freed me up from many limitations. It has made a big difference in my life, but the scars and injuries I experienced while I had epilepsy will say with me and unfortunately the damage caused will never heal nor will I be able to make up for what I have been robbed of by the state.

I am trying to put my experiences into some form of theory or analogy which when taken on board can be applied generally to the many who cannot speak up for or defend themselves and therefore give some insight into how widespread the problem is and then to determine how much of this neglect and abuse of vulnerable individuals is really going on.

In 1960 I was born with scar tissue on the brain which developed into temporal lobe epilepsy in 1973. This was induced by complications as I was born a month premature and forceps are believed to have caused the bruising on my head. I had minor problems throughout early childhood but the real problem started when I was twelve and it lasted through to the age of thirty-five.

What came with it was a gift for mathematics – I understood some mathematical ideas worthy of A-level which I had devised for myself before going to secondary school – that was without any private tuition, mentoring or support other than what I was taught in primary school. I was known for my imagination and brainpower but all this was ignored by people in positions of authority throughout the time I had epilepsy as I was labelled as subnormal. I now see these people who undermined me so much like cowards on The Weakest Link looking for whatever excuse they can to make stronger look weaker so they can be in control and appear better than they really are.

Childhood was not easy with external limitations and bullying including poverty. Many problems were external and the epilepsy didn't really restrict me from using my potential - all it did was inconvenience me for a short time while I had a seizure and needed time to recover.

This time amounted to less than one per cent of the total time so for ninety-nine per cent of the time I was more active and capable than the average person. But people used this small glitch in my life to treat me as if I was incapable 24/7/365. I managed to go to college & university and got a degree in mathematics. I wouldn't be limited by others trying to impose restrictions on my activities even though the state betrayed me by refusing to help me, a gifted individual from a disadvantaged background, make the most of my potential and therefore I underperformed.

This is typical of the state failing the disadvantaged gifted, and throughout the twenty years I was living in the Bridgend area of South Wales with uncontrolled epilepsy I didn't receive a single penny for my care needs from Social Security as they fraudulently denied me my entitlements. Not knowing how corrupt civil servants were at the time I didn't question this and accepted what I was told as I was given the impression I had to be either a cripple or mentally retarded to get support.

Every seizure came a short warning (aura) - about half a minute minimum, so could get to safety. This gave me time to prepare myself as it wasn't sudden and so I exploited this to get more freedom. Sometimes I would cycle to and from college – twenty miles each way – partly for the enjoyment and partly to save money (bus fare) as times were hard and any extras were obtained by sacrifices.

If I had a seizure I would rest for about twenty minutes and then continue my journey and all it would result in was a minor delay. I always allowed extra time in the morning for this not to be late but the unexpected could happen. Sometimes I would have a seizure in the afternoon not long before home time e.g. having a seizure at 3 pm, and at home time I would start the twenty miles cycle home at the end of the day – normally about 4 pm. People showed concern about getting me home safely but I knew my capabilities and I would be safe. Eventually they accepted me for this and knew I could manage it.

After graduating with a degree in maths I could not get employment worthy of my qualifications as no employer wanted me in spite of my mathematical abilities and the temporal lobe epilepsy affecting me less than one per cent of the total time. Even though ninety nine per cent of my capability is more than one hundred per cent of an average person's capability I was rejected everywhere.

Eventually I was forced to take a job with the Mid Glamorgan Social Services Department (MGSSD) which was worse than school leaver's level with minimal O-levels/CSEs and I had a degree. If I refused this offer I would have had my benefit stopped so I was held to ransom by the unscrupulous public services. The seeds of doubt which were planted in me back in 1973 had fully established themselves within me and the roots were very deep now.

For almost eight years this authority exploited me for my talents and paid me pittance for my efforts. Like cowards on The Weakest Link being exploited for production but treated as the weakest when it came to reward for what I had done, it tried all it could to get the most out of me with the minimal of reward.

As time went by my behaviour started to get problematic and I would regularly be at loggerheads with my boss. Personally, because there was no positive future ahead I didn't care if I ended up getting sacked, and over time people noticed the deterioration of my character. I had nothing to lose and if times had not improved I may have become so problematic that my career prospects would have been ruined and I may have ended up institutionalised. I eventually appeared in a documentary called Same Difference on Channel 4 regarding exploitation and discrimination of individuals like me after news of how I had been treated like started to get out, but MGSSD refused to be interviewed.

It is obvious that this was not genuine discrimination but epilepsy being used as a tool to undermine me because those responsible were useless currants. If they couldn't see that I was more capable than the average person, then they are obsessed and narrow-minded in some way, and as this is was oppression they are wicked for abusing my rights and trying to destroy my life.

If they had seen me as less capable they wouldn't have tried to restrict me like they did, so it is obvious they tried to make me look incapable and subjected me to years of oppression in an attempt to prevent me from progressing. My progress was held to ransom by these control freaks – without them I was stronger so when they interfered I was weakened. Therefore I wasn't weak; they were the weakest links in my chain which weakened me.

If I was what the authorities had claimed I would have got some help; or if I was accepted as gifted I would also have had some help. But the way I was treated suggests the authorities knew I was gifted and had exceptional talent but didn't want to accept me for what I was and wanted to make me feel inadequate and destroy my progress.

So all the restrictions were used to force me into a lower category and hopefully you will see their objectives to turn me into a failure failed and now we know that I was treated like this because I was too good for them.

So if they did this to me, how many others are persecuted and treated like dirt and restricted from progressing at their natural rate because they are too good for the control freaks in authority?

Throughout this time of restriction I would get away from my problems by cycling and taking the bike on the train to various locations around the UK – mostly England & Wales on my own. I needed to get away to somewhere I wasn't known and was prepared in case I had a seizure and needed help. I got further around the country with my bike and public transport than many who had a car.

Medication was unable to control the epilepsy and caused me behavioural problems so neurologists decided that if it was safe for me to have brain surgery then it would be the only option for improving the quality of my life. After undergoing brain surgery the results weren't immediate. It took a while to adjust to a new way of life and convincing myself that the operation was a full success. Eventually I started to enjoy life more and appreciate my freedom.

So given the way the abuse and betrayal I experienced have affected my behaviour and how I have been labelled, I have grounds to believe that many disadvantaged youngsters from poor backgrounds who have been betrayed by the state and end up getting labelled as “delinquents” are victims and not wrongdoers when they haven’t been given a fair chance, a voice or been listened to and so they end up like this through betrayal and neglect as none of this is their fault.

They are often deprived of a fair deal and whenever they try to speak out they are punished more so the majority are disadvantaged and blamed for others faults like I was. So I wonder if the majority of those who end up as “criminals” have been driven this way through persecution by the authorities. People in authority are responsible for wrecking many lives and since they never listen or learn from their failings I am pretty sure it is intentional in many cases.

It is only because I saw the chance to move forward by fighting the system (rather disruptively) and have secured my freedom from this stranglehold that the better side of me has started to come out again, although not anywhere near as good as it was prior to when all the abuse started in 1973.

So I am lucky (if you can call it that) to have escaped, but had there been no opportunity to move on then I could have continued as I was or even ended up inside and labelled as a criminal or mentally disturbed when I was wholly innocent being a victim of abuse, scarred by the experiences and driven into desperation. If I wasn’t able to escape I may have ended up as a criminal after being treated worse than one for so many years with no hope of ever moving on.

I wouldn’t be surprised if this is what the control freaks want since they drive the majority of victims along this line so they can appear spotless with what they are doing when they are deliberately colluding with others to cause problems for the vulnerable in order to side-track any attention from their wrongdoings.

I believe that those in authority when I was living in the Bridgend area tried to drive me towards committing suicide in order to keep what happened quiet. Could there be some link to the Bridgend suicide victims and abuse by control freaks in authority? They are like cowards on The Weakest Link who gang up and use their votes to make the strongest look the weakest by using politics and bureaucracy to make trustworthy, reliable strong individuals look untrustworthy, unreliable and weak - because goodness and the truth is not in their interest.

There were cheats, liars and backstabbers out there trying to stay on top and control society and so when you have this type in power you will always get charlatans controlling society through abuse of power and wrongdoing while persecuting the decent and glamorising the wicked.

As I have now rebuilt my life, I help vulnerable individuals (children and the elderly); I have tutored children from disadvantaged backgrounds in maths to help make it more interesting which has been successful as some have broken the barrier which prevented them understanding the subject. I am also involved in singing (a baritone where I am tenor or bass as required), an actor for amateur dramatics and other organisations.

Unfortunately I haven't had the choice of going into a career where I would have made the most of my potential so have had to accept a reduced choice. There are so many I could have slotted into but I wasn't considered because of all the labelling instead of being seen for my potential, so why do some people look for "faults" like discrimination in gifted individuals? Probably because of their Cowards on The Weakest Link mentality - ones who get where they are under false pretences and others who are genuine are a threat to their false one-upmanship.

If I was what the authorities labelled me as when I lived in the Bridgend area I wouldn't be where I am now, so based on how they restricted my progress, I question what do the authorities in the Bridgend area do to the disadvantaged now since it became the suicide capital of the UK? If they cannot invest in the potential of someone with a medical condition that has exceptional mathematical abilities and can be fully active for more than 99% of the time then it can only be said that the bureaucratic impropriety in the public services and the exercising of false one-upmanship by those in positions of authority are responsible for failing many vulnerable people for their own selfish greed and egotism.

Some argue that I am trying to say the world owes me a living mostly by those who expect more than they deserve at others expense. I am not claiming that the world owes me a living - I am claiming that the state has defrauded and conned me out of plenty as well as having denied me my rights, freedom of choice and my entitlements so it owes me a lot. So as I have been robbed of plenty I am owed a lot due to failure by the state.

If I don't deserve what I claim to have been robbed of, why do so many deserve so much more for not trying but expecting to live of the state with no special care needs or talents when I tried to use my potential to the full but wasn't let?

I shall always be living in residual poverty since I am paying the price for all this betrayal and not living the quality of life I should have had if I had the opportunities I deserved.

It is quite likely I would have had much better quality of life at a lower price, better pay, a bigger house and would have paid my mortgage by now and thus more disposable income and enjoying life a lot more; but I have to accept less and on lower income, and will be in debt until I retire. Some people on Social Security are living in more luxury with all their bills paid.

If I had been given equal opportunities and this hadn't been accomplished, then I could say it was misfortune or my fault; but how I have been treated and conned means it is the state which has caused all this. So I shall never forgive the state for what it has done to my overall quality of life regarding abuse, betrayal, neglect and unfairness. I shall always hate the authorities for what they have done and how they can get away with it and come out squeaky clean; so such people responsible for these actions deserve to be named and shamed – individually or by department.

If I had been given a fair chance and failed then it could say it was my fault; but because I wasn't given a fair chance and I have been significantly stronger without their domination and interference this is proof the authorities were the weakest links in my life and therefore held me to ransom and also caused the residual poverty I will have for the remainder of my life.

So with this fact proving I am a victim of abuse of power it will fuel my rage at people in authority who abuse their power to come out on top and avoid the truth. I will never be to blame for my behaviour after how I was treated and the stubbornness I experience against the truth which has nurtured me into being so disruptive when I feel under threat.

All my problems were caused by useless currants in positions of authority and whenever I get into dispute with anyone it is because someone is trying to force me to suffer for their gains. So I am never to blame for any conflicts and if the authorities treat me inappropriately I will do what I can to name and shame them.

If I ever get into trouble it will be one of the worst things anyone in authority does to me because it will spill the beans on many more incidents of abuse and how I was treated as well as why they continue to treat me the way they do and all the attempts to suppress the truth.

Why are there so many small people standing on higher platforms trying to make out they are bigger because their head is above ours when they are really smaller? If they were standing on the same level they would be smaller.

They all have some form of little person syndrome (or Napoleon Complex) trying to make out they are better than they really are and in order to maintain their false one-upmanship they have to abuse those of us who are a threat to their false standards. They feel inadequate to have the desire to make better individuals look worse and bring us down to below their level.

I believe that we have psychopaths in control of society to suppress the development and progress of many so that a selective clique of glorified simpletons and privileged psychopaths can rule society. Those who are unsympathetic towards the disadvantaged and treat them as if they deserve this are likely to be jealous because they are less capable and cannot accept the truth for what they are. The disadvantaged are seen as an opportunity for those psychopaths to hide their faults behind.

Many appear to exhibit behaviour that is consistent with symptoms associated with a medical disorder known as psychopathy. Psychopaths, also called sociopaths, are categorized as those who exhibit superficial charm and intelligence, and are absent of delusions or nervousness. Their traits include:

- A frequent need for excitement
- A need for complete power
- A need to dominate others
- An ability to rationalize their behaviour
- An inflated self-worth
- Antisocial behaviour
- Deceitful and manipulative behaviour (either goal-oriented or for the delight of the act itself)
- Frequent lying
- Incapacity for love
- Lack of remorse or shame
- Loss of insight
- Poor judgment and failure to learn by experience
- Poverty of general emotions
- Unreliability
- Unresponsiveness in personal relations

So they look for excuses to bring us down; we are already recognised and so don't have to achieve anything else or succeed with our careers – we simply want a fair deal in life and if we get exposed to persecution by abusers or don't get a fair share we will quite happily refuse to deliver our qualities and therefore sink to the bottom behaving in accordance with how we are being treated. That means if we are treated worse than others then you can expect us to behave worse than others – mostly in the way of defence and retaliation to how we are being treated.

No matter how badly we behave, this won't make any difference to our capabilities or invalidate the fact that we have proven our natural giftedness which the majority of them haven't got.

How many professors in Oxford or Cambridge could do some A-level maths on their own in junior school without any private tuition or mentoring? Being able to do this proves I have more capability than being a professor at Oxford or Cambridge, so I don't care what snob value they have. I haven't been given a chance to do well – probably because the snobby don't like poorer individuals from disadvantaged backgrounds doing better because it makes the snobs look false.

Only if they could do what I could in junior school without any extra support I would accept them as being on the same tier as me; so generally they are likely to be on a lower tier naturally but put on a higher tier through privileges. There is no genuine tier above what I am on so they have no reason to look down at me other than for snob value purposes.

Snob value is nothing more than a smokescreen by the privileged and wealthy to cover up their weaknesses they do not wish to have disclosed or be seen with in public; so they use snob value to evade competition and exposure of their weaknesses. If they exercise snobbery, there is usually something they are trying to hide.

People at the top have too much say on what goes on in society and if they want to suppress our progress or have preferential treatment they can get this quite easily as they have more say. As individuals they shouldn't have any more say than anyone else – they should only have more say in what affects their private life and stays within their own world; not on the control of others' lives.

"I am proud to be a survivor and having risen above many who mocked me and tried to ruin my life; but because they couldn't rise above me they had the desire to bring me down to below their level and in doing so subjected me to years of oppression, abuse and all sorts of acts of negativity associated with inabilities on their side. So I have shown double success – survived much more than they have ever endured; and much more capable than all the spoon-feeding and cheating they need to elevate themselves and exercise false one-upmanship on many of us. They must have been really desperate and feel really down as they have failed in their mission as well as having given me the chance to prove I am even better than I would have shown has I been let get on with my life."

"The truth will never change and those who have tried to make me scapegoat for their faults and weaknesses will never be any stronger no matter how much status, wealth or anything external they have – the weakest link in their lives is themselves. It is nice to know they will permanently be held prisoner by their inabilities and cannot bring their victims down permanently to their level. I don't aim to be at the top since the top aren't essentially the best and it is more a must for the pretentious than the genuine. I want to live life to the full and am happy where I am in relation to the population rather than worrying about where I am in relation to other individuals. I am also living proof that individuals treated at the bottom can have better capabilities and more potential than many who are perched on the top."

So if they attempt to ruin some of us for being too good, why do we have such people in positions of authority and trust when they abuse the rights of the vulnerable or do something they believe they will get away with and never be found out? If they managed to prevent me from progressing they would have still been seen in the right and the truth about my potential would never have come out.

One thing to bear in mind and think about is that the control freaks in positions of trust and power behind all neglect of the vulnerable always have to be seen as innocent until proven guilty; but they treat all of us they wish to undermine as guilty until proven innocent. This means they are seen whiter than white until they are found out, but because we are seen as guilty until proven innocent we aren't listened to and anything we complain about is ignored and treated worthy of lies, which consequently means none of us get any right to justice and support worthy of what we deserve as this assumed label of being guilty gets us seen as in the wrong all the time. It is only because I broke away from the stranglehold and proved that they were holding me to ransom I have managed to prove I was innocent, but I am still not properly listened to and the government departments and bodies guilty of contributing towards what I was put through are desperate to keep me silenced so they can continue to be seen as innocent until proven guilty hoping that the opportunity to prove their guilt never materialises. Well this book is a way around that as information on how I was treated proves that.

None of this is intended to target normal individuals in general who have achieved success through proper channels or are at a disadvantage and less capable. It is aimed at those who are cheats, liars, backstabbers, abusers and behave in perverted ways abusing their positions of trust and authority – mostly ones who have a desire to win at all expenses by destroying the chances of those who are better and wanting control of everything so that they can have a better quality of life at the expense of others – mostly the disadvantaged and vulnerable because they cannot stick up for themselves and these abusers are too afraid to do this to stronger individuals and it shows they are like cowards on The Weakest Link as they wouldn't win if they challenged their victims face-to-face or on a one-to-one basis. They have to use external support, tools, resources and power of authority which they abuse to come out on top. The best are never recognised properly because we are too good for the brains of the privileged and corrupt whose desire it is to come out on top at all costs.

You will see that those who are false and exercise false one-upmanship cannot be in control forever as they have to be on guard all the time to suppress the progress of others who have the potential to break away and go further. That is how I got away from their stranglehold and the truth has come out of their failed attempts.

Due to not being listened to and ignored by many of the authorities and organisations supposed to help vulnerable people, this book is a last resort for to get myself heard and even if my book is ignored by ones responsible for failing the vulnerable, many others will read about my ordeals. Those in authority who have hidden behind the walls of bureaucracy and been sheltered by whatever means will know something has come out even if they don't want to read about it. It doesn't matter whether they accept it or not, the fact is that some of the truth has come out.

Have you noticed that the scum always rises to the top as well as rot coming out on top? Maybe this is nature's way of showing that those at the top are more liken to be rot than decent? Read on and you will see what really goes on. This is where inferiority is used to destroy others' lives.

I am a member of Lions Clubs International, a worldwide charity which helps disadvantaged people and offered various amounts of support to disadvantaged people in and outside of Lions Clubs International. But like very organisation, there will always be someone who won't accept me for what I am and although I was someone who could have done with some support when I needed it the most, some members were interested and say I am a role model in setting an example, whereas others hold their nose up at me and don't want to know me because I am someone who thinks individually and won't be led by others. Some seem to see me as a troublemaker than a victim.

Well, facts cannot contradict facts; opinions can contradict opinions where there is a clash; but opinions are often used to try to contradict facts while facts are used in defence against opinionated contradictions generated by the rot at the top. Opinions have no factual weight as they don't have to be based around fact. So rather than give opinions which are factually based more credit than those with no factual base, all opinions have no factual weight. It is the fact which is present (if so) which has the weight, not the opinion. I don't like results which don't reflect the truth – and especially dislike those which invert the truth. Only when amends have been made and the result reflects he truth will I accept it.

Results never reflect the truth whenever an inferiority factor is involved as this is quite likely to invert the truth and make small look bigger than big.

Inferiority is a term I used which is an internal comparison of what someone really is in comparison with the image they like to be seen as, so if someone is pretentious trying to appear better than they really are then they are inferior to their image and this inferiority is where a lot of problems within society originate since such people cannot progress without being destructive to others. It is not a comparison between individuals as we all have strengths and weaknesses – it exists when a deliberate attempt of false one-upmanship is exercised. I can often identify inferiority in people who try to make me a victim of their false one-upmanship and I will do what I can to make it backfire on them.

I might be the little man in the street when it comes to those with status and wealth; but I am in no way as weak as them when it comes to natural potential.

So term 'too good' doesn't mean I am trying to put myself on a pedestal but it means I was too good for what they were prepared to accept me as; and even being slightly brighter than average would be too good for those who tried to label me as subnormal and couldn't accept the truth. They weren't prepared to accept me as being above them when they wanted me to be seen below them; so I was too good for what they were prepared to accept.

Many vulnerable people are 'too good' for what those in authority are prepared to accept them as since they are often labelled in an insulting way and if they are better they are often subjected to abuse. This is where I use the phrases 'Evils of inferiority' and 'Inflictions of inferiority' since they are all destructive and evil. So being gifted must have really put the rage in them and this is probably why their intentions were to destroy my progress and make me feel inadequate. From the beginning I could see that the small people in authority were trying to make bigger individuals from disadvantaged backgrounds look even smaller, and the only way they could do this to us was to abuse, betray, neglect and persecute those of us they weren't prepared to accept.

It must be very frustrating that there are far too many ordinary individuals within society who are too good for the sick and twisted individuals in positions of power who want to be in control.

Background & Experiences

1. Birth & Early Days

My mother was a State Registered Nurse and my father a Sergeant in the RAF. They met in Ely, Cambridgeshire and eventually were based at RAF Swanton Morley in Norfolk. My mother was told that it was quite unlikely that she would be able to have a baby but I somehow came into this world so she did have one big baby - me.

In 1960 she succeeded in becoming pregnant and I was born at a hospital in Norwich after eight months and weighed eight pounds and four ounces. Due to my size my mother had complications and during this process the forceps bruised my head which caused scar tissue on the brain and later caused epilepsy. The bruising went away after a few days I was told but that is where the scar tissue was which left me with epilepsy for many years. So it appears my brain injury was caused by the NHS as the bruising was fresh and just what forceps would have caused if used incorrectly.

There didn't appear to be any problems in my early years and all went well or so it seemed. As a baby I wouldn't be bottle-fed but only accepted being breast fed. I have never liked milk and have always gone out of my way to avoid it. As time went by, I would refuse cereal and starve myself than have breakfast if milk was added.

I didn't like to be spoon-fed either (in more ways than one). I was very curious to find things out for myself and appreciate the roots than take too much for granted. I found water very fascinating and did a lot with water. Later I took an interest in meteorology (the weather) and still do now.

My father was a keen rugby player and was known for his skills. One day though he was involved in an accident which ruptured his liver and had to be invalided out of the RAF. Unfortunately in 1964 he died.

2. The Loss Of My Father

We moved from Swanton Morley in Norfolk to Kenfig Hill, near Bridgend in South Wales, where my father was brought up. His liver became infected and sadly he passed away in September 1964 and was buried in St James Church in Pyle. This left just my mother and me.

My father was a very calm and well-liked person of whom many said he was one of the nicest they had come across. One friend Herbert Martin who missed him wanted to do something in return for what he did as a friend and in 2013 had a gravestone done for his grave.

I was quite a keen and playful child and got on well with the neighbours and friends but my mother wanted to return to her place of upbringing which was Coventry, so we moved there.

3. Junior Days Before Epilepsy

After moving to the Hillfields area of Coventry we settled down but I was very advanced for my age. I lived in Hillfields House in Yardley Street and several shops nearby were Philips' Hardware, Porter's Newsagents and De-Diez Ice Cream. One day while at infants school a crane involved with the construction of the flats opposite between Nelson Street and Wellington Street came down and went into nearby houses on Nelson Street. A girl in my class Mary Wilson lived in one of these houses.

As I settled down I was enthusiastic and wanted to do more than I was allowed. Suppressing my enthusiasm didn't go down well with me - I became more determined to defy those in authority for punishing or undermining me for trying as I was being told off more than the troublemakers. This was reflected in school where one teacher who was rather aggressive and incompetent picked on me a bit because I was too bright for her liking.

I was also undermined by some members of the family on my mother's side who later took advantage to label me as schizophrenic when I started having epilepsy. They looked for every opportunity to undermine me. I have tried to see the good in them but they have never accepted me or shown concern for the abuse I suffered over the years but treated me as if I was an outcast and deserved to be abused.

Gifted individuals also have a high level of emotional intelligence and very often my emotional intelligence was mistaken for being troublesome. I used to get worked up when I disagreed with people of higher authority who were automatically assumed to be in the right and I was in the wrong when I knew I was right and so I wasn't going to let the truth be overruled by authority or as I would say, "Inversion of the truth".

To get some understanding on how emotional intelligence and feelings play a part, take a look at this website as it explains a lot which backs up my theories. It is based in Australia since nothing has been available on this level in the UK. It reads:

Giftedness has an emotional as well as an intellectual component: gifted children not only think differently from their peers, they also feel differently. This difference in feeling is emotional intensity; a positive force for the gifted that feeds, enriches, empowers and amplifies talent.

http://www.giftedservices.com.au/index.html

Unfortunately some teachers wouldn't let me feel enriched with my emotional intensity but treated it as if it was a form of troublemaking and became very negative towards my giftedness.

I was never one who wanted to cause problems for others - I just wanted to maximise my potential and sometimes I had to fight others who were trying to subject me to oppression. People in authority were the biggest culprits because "they know best". Huh - they are control freaks with no knowledge of what it is like to be gifted. So if they tried to suppress my progress I would work my way round but if they became aggressive and restricting treating me in the wrong for wanting to progress I would put up a fight.

You will see how my emotional intensity got me involved in big arguments with people in authority including teachers and the occasional fight.

i. St Mary's Infants' School, Gosford Green

In 1965 in my first year in infants' school less than a year after my father died, I went to St. Mary's Infants' School near Gosford Green in Coventry and the teachers at the time included Miss Jackson, Mrs Murray, Mr Ledbetter (Mr Bed Wetter), Mr Wheeler and the headmaster Mr Gunter. There were others but I didn't have anything to do with those.

Milk was provided at break time but I never wanted to touch the stuff.

Later on during my first year in infants' school in 1966 (less than two years after my father passed away), the teacher Miss Jackson was a nasty piece of work. She was doing some arithmetic on the blackboard and I noticed she had made a mistake. I tried to point out the mistake but she wouldn't accept it - but I knew she had. She had difficulty in convincing me that I was wrong because I knew she was wrong.

I got so fed up of her lies I got up from my desk, went up to the blackboard, rubbed out her mistake and corrected it in front of the class.

After this, she didn't like me and knowing I didn't like milk she forced me to drink a bottle at break time - it was a form of punishment for sticking up for myself and not letting a teacher abuse her power of position to make something wrong look right.

I was most upset and was in tears so didn't go to the toilet like I normally did at break time. About half way through class I needed to go to the toilet - for two reasons:

- I hadn't gone at break time like I normally did due to being upset; and
- I had consumed some milk and I normally don't have anything to drink at break time.

So I tried to get her attention but she ignored me. I was in need of going so I persisted but she continued to ignore me, so after asking her many times I heard her say "Yes" which I took to mean I could go to the toilet, so I went.

When I got back she questioned me where I had gone and why I did it without permission. I tried to say that I did ask permission and she said yes, but she wouldn't have it. I believe she deliberately did this to mislead me so she could punish me when I got back.

She hit me hard with the ruler and humiliated me in front of the class. I was so outraged I raised my voice at her and was sent to have the cane. I did this and was only five years of age so it destroyed my trust in people with authority so I have never fully trusted teachers who are aggressive and try to abuse their power of authority to override the truth. I also started to use my voice quite firmly and now have quite a distinguished voice.

Christopher Kelly remembers some of this.

This type of abuse was seen as discipline in these days, so I found out in 2012 when I was encouraged to report the abuse I had experienced when the floodgates opened after Jimmy Savile's actions came to light. Today this behaviour by teachers wouldn't be tolerated.

So damage beyond repair was caused in my first year in school and I have never had trust in teachers that exercise control and aggression over the children and always have to be right when they cannot understand the child. I have targeted some teachers like this throughout my school days as I don't like being belittled by someone in charge who is intellectually inferior in order to come out on top.

This was the start of many canings for answering her back (and many other teachers who treated me inappropriately). I had the cane nearly every other day or at least twice a week for answering her back. I felt this wasn't discipline but punishment for not letting those in control decide what is right and letting wrongdoing be seen as right.

So I started having the cane regularly when I was only five years old - when I was defending myself from an aggressive and undermining teacher. Had she not treated me like this I wouldn't have had any cause for punishment as I never got into trouble with the other children. I wasn't afraid of anyone in authority as I saw them as bullies in control when they were nasty and unfair and I told them what I thought. I became a bit problematic knowing I had been abused for doing things properly. I wasn't going to let a "thick" teacher pull me down to below her level and so I was always catching her out and became too much for her. I made it difficult for he and I was only five years old. It serves her right for trying to hide her weakness behind me as a child.

If she had respected me I would have respected her but because of what she did to me and how she used me I couldn't help but wish her dead. This shows how abusing a child can result in years of disruptive behaviour as you will see.

Mary, my step grandmother who was my mother's step mother (since my true grandmother died when my mother was a child) never accepted my mother or me and always looked for faults. She would threaten to scald me with a kettle of boiling water if I didn't do what she wanted. I was just enthusiastic to find out more, not troublesome which she didn't like. She saw my defence against being emotionally abused by teachers as being unruly claiming it was discipline and I deserved it.

In 1968 my mother was concerned that I wasn't getting the education I needed for my potential so she tried to get me into another school. Some of the family were starting to shun me because I was progressing too much and they saw it as wrong. I would stand up for myself and speak out which they didn't like.

ii. St Bede's School, Bishton Hall

Regarding my education there were two options - a boarding school where I would come home at weekends or one where we would put all our belongings into store and she would become matron while I was a pupil at the school and we would both reside there. We decided to go for the latter and this school was St Bede's School at Bishton Hall in Wolseley Bridge near Stafford which has been owned by the Stafford-Northcote family for generations. We started at St Bede's in September 1968.

Our time at St Bede's was a bit unstable as we had nowhere to live during the holidays as our belongings were in store, and so had to regularly look for temporary accommodation. During the holidays we either stayed in the area or with relatives in Hemel Hempstead. This gave me the opportunity to do a bit of walking around the Wolseley Bridge, Colwich, Little/Great Haywood, Shugborough, Milford, Colton, Rugeley and other nearby areas. I regularly drive around these places when passing the area to reminisce and see how things have changed.

Although I liked it, my mother felt that it was too snooty and although a pupil at the school we couldn't afford what the other pupils had so I was left out a bit. So in the autumn term of 1969 my mother had been looking at resigning and getting me into another school, so this was where we relocated to South Wales again.

iii. St Joseph's Convent, Clydach-On-Tawe

In January 1970 I was a border at St Joseph's convent in Clydach-on-Tawe near Swansea for a term while my mother sorted out some accommodation/housing for us. I experienced some emotional abuse by one teacher a nun Sister Finton who was aggressive and strict - like Miss Jackson and she regularly used a large cane to poke children with to get their attention.

Finton was quite nasty and so I had some exchanges of words with her and one day she became quite aggressive with her threats and I told her if she touches me she will get this (showing her my fist at her face). Finton was a fat, grumpy, overweight lump who enjoyed bullying children.

I was the most unruly of all children at the school/convent. But then it looks like when you get abused and retaliate they will try to make the retaliation look like you are unruly and try to scare you into keeping quiet - but I wasn't one to be silenced and will keep on until the matter has been resolved. I was only there for one term.

iv. Mynydd Cynffig Junior School, Kenfig Hill

After Easter in 1970 when we got some temporary accommodation in Kenfig Hill so I went to Mynydd Cynffig Junior School for a term. There was no abuse or negativity - I was just outperforming others and accepted for it.

I was a bit inquisitive and can remember Mr Morgan who was the headmaster. I was in his study trying to negotiate better opportunities for me as I was outperforming other children. He had what looked like a light switch on the end of a lead hanging down from the ceiling and I thought it was a light. I pressed it and a bell rang which caused some panic.

I was then moved up to the next year as I was too bright for those of the same academic age. It was easier for me but I didn't like feeling special. I was only there for one term.

v. St Joseph's RC Junior School, Port Talbot

During the summer of 1970 we got a maisonette in North Cornelly and I went to St. Joseph's Junior School in Port Talbot for a term up to Christmas. I didn't get on too well with some of the teachers but there was no abuse. They were too grumpy and I didn't feel welcome, so we looked at going to another junior school. I had the cane for something I didn't do so after this I never had trust in the school and wanted to leave. I was only there for one term.

vi. Corneli Junior School, North Cornelly

In January 1971 I started at Corneli County Junior School and settled down very well. I got on with all the other children but got bullied a bit by outsiders from neighbouring areas on the estates as the estates were rundown council estates and poverty was rife. At least I managed to move on and this was the last school I went to before problems really did start.

For the remaining two terms of the academic year and the last year of my junior school days I was starting to move on and during this time I could understand some maths worthy of A-level standard without any private tuition or mentoring. I had thought these ideas out myself but because I had nobody with advanced knowledge with me I wasn't properly recognised for it. I was recognised as being outstanding and just though t of my ideas as maths which I would come across later in school but only when I did A-level maths later did I realise what I was doing I knew in junior school. As a matter of fact, Einstein and Newton had mentors for support during their younger years but I didn't get any extra support. My mother wasn't a mathematician so I did everything myself and thought these ideas up myself. This is something I can claim above Einstein and Newton because I did it without any additional support, so what if I got support and recognition like they had from an early age?

The teacher Mr Jones really did recognise my talent and was one of the most supportive of teachers I had. He didn't give me preferential treatment but respected me for my abilities. The report showed how well I can behave when treated accordingly which is a lot different to how I have turned out due to abuse I have experienced and all the undermining too.

This was the last true reflection of my true capabilities since seven months later I started having temporal lobe epilepsy and have always been treated as less deserving and of lower capability than the average person because of all the discrimination I have experienced. What they are really saying is that I haven't had as much spoon-feeding as others and this is what they go by. I have a genuine connection with mathematical genius which no person of normal intelligence on this planet has irrespective of not having the chance to make the most of my potential. It is like filling a bigger jug with less than a smaller jug doesn't make its capacity less – but that is what the less capable want to see so they can make small look bigger than big.

The actor Owen Teale was a pupil at this school when I was there and was a friend. He was known as Tull.

During this time I was also referred to a child psychiatrist Dr Hartley at Tynygarn Clinic, near Aberkenfig who I saw every term to discuss my progress and the bullying I was getting. It wasn't to do with the school but mostly older children (teenagers) trying to bring me down and making out I was at fault because I was different.

My report in July 1972 below when I finished junior school.

Glamorgan Education Authority

Corneli Junior School

Report on pupil's work for the year ending July 1972

NAME ***John Ricades*** CLASS ***6***

Subject		GRADE Effort	GRADE Attainment	Remarks
English	Oral	***B***	***B***	Attendance ***V Good***
	Written	***B+***	***B+***	
English Reading		***B+***	***B+***	Punctuality ***V Good***
Mathematics		***A***	***A***	Conduct ***Good***
Welsh		***C+***	***C***	Progress ***V Good***
Local Studies		***C+***	***C+***	General Report ***A very capable boy who has been most cooperative during the year.***
Art		***C***	***C***	
Craft		***C+***	***C+***	
Physical Activities		***C***	***C***	Attitude to Work ***V Good***

Grades	A	Excellent	***He has good all-round ability but is particularly good in maths at which he could go a long way.***
	B+	Very Good	
	B	Good/Above Average	
	C	Average	
	D	Fair	School re-opens for the Autumn Term On
	E	Slow	

Signed ***B J Jones*** Class Teacher ***B R Hare*** Head Teacher

4. The First Few Years Of Epilepsy - Life Goes Downhill From Here

i. Mynydd Cynffig Comprehensive School, Kenfig Hill

In September 1972 I started at Mynydd Cynffig Comprehensive School and it was a very emotional move. Bullying became unbearable and whenever I complained to teachers I was shouted at and told off.

Every day I was being bullied and I felt unhappy at going to school. Sometimes I would refuse to go to school and create saying it wasn't safe for me with all the bullying I was experiencing.

So we just had to put up with it and the regular disturbing stories of bullying I had when I came home every day nearly always crying.

ii. Diagnosed With Epilepsy

In February 1973 I had the mumps and not long after it had my first epileptic fit of which I was finally labelled as epileptic. Hormonal changes were starting to take place within the body so the chemical imbalance probably triggered it. I was also put on a cocktail of drugs which affected my behaviour and was of no help.

This chemical imbalance together with the bullying I was experiencing combined with the shock and trauma of having epilepsy and being over restricted didn't provide a stable environment for me and I felt things were going out of hand. I was treated abruptly by staff and people from the local authority as if I was causing trouble when I was defending myself and I had no control over my seizures. I didn't want to be restricted as if I was less capable than others because I had epilepsy but everyone in authority tried to suppress my progress.

Circumstances were getting out of hand with bullying, trauma, blame and more together with no support but what appeared to be punishment for everything which had gone wrong and I was getting fed up with life.

iii. Education Offices, Minerva Street, Bridgend

On Monday 12th March 1973 my mother and I went to the local authority offices in Minerva Street to sort something out for me. While my mother was in seeing an officer I was waiting and getting a bit fed up, so I wandered along the corridor looking at posters and notices on the walls.

Unfortunately doing this was wrong because an aggressive woman (like Miss Jackson and Sister Finton) came out and raised her voice at me for not remaining seated and quizzed me what I was doing.

She spoke to me in an aggressive tone of voice and tried to catch me out. I was seen as wrong from every angle and wasn't given the chance to speak or defend myself so I lost control of my temper and emotions and went berserk.

Being spoken to in an inappropriate tone of voice, treated as in the wrong for not remaining seated, humiliated in front of others, etc. by a pretentious jobsworth of a worker was the final straw and a change of personality. From this day on I have left a trail of violence and destruction in my path in retaliation of how I have been treated.

Since then I have never respected anyone who speaks to me in the wrong tone of voice and raised my voice in return at them. I have answered many back in an assertive voice in front of others for treating me inappropriately and it has certainly humiliated some people with long term psychological effects - serves them right for trying to use me. Many have been shamed in front of others and couldn't come to terms with it.

It goes to show how devastating it can be to a child who is being abused when he or she is trying to be listened to and some self-important jumped-up bossy cow in authority who wants to look in control treats the victim inappropriately. This woman who treated me inappropriately when I was innocent caused me to flip. it shows how much had bottled up in me not being listened to so when I was punished for being 100% innocent it changed my personality for the worst for the rest of my life and it is still present today if I am victimised. anyone who talks to me inappropriately in a tone of voice like she did gets me ready for battle with them and once my temper and emotions start coming out of my voice it certainly gets attention and creates panic.

This was the start of a trail of destruction which has been going on for over forty years. Also, this was about the peak when many children in care homes were being abused by staff, so I experienced abuse through bullying and control tactics.

My behaviour was out-of-character as I am not normally this way. It was a combination of abuse, bulling, betrayal, fear and trauma which made me become violent as this violence was a form of defence and a need for survival. It shows the extent someone will go to survive and I was a bit too much for anyone to handle without physical force, so I used this destructive potential I realised I had in defence and revenge on people who tried to abuse me. They would never be able to control me without using an element of control associated with abuse of power as you will see, so over the years I have left a trail of destruction but never got into trouble because it was always in defence.

Unfortunately this experience has changed my personality and character for the worse and was the start of what has become of a trail of destruction lasting over forty years. It is all linked to the evils of inferiority associated with the abuse and use of status, wealth, power, authority and control; and I will not let these factors invert the truth against me without a fight.

iv. Pen-y-fai Hospital, Bridgend

As a result of this sudden loss of control of all my emotions and temper, I started tearing off my clothes, throwing anything I could pick up out of my way and leaving a trail of destruction in my path, you could see that something wasn't right so I was rushed to Tynygarn Clinic to see Dr Hartley who then admitted me into Pen-y-fai Adults Psychiatric Hospital and I was only twelve years of age. I had to be sedated with Valium and locked up in a cell to calm down. This was the start of years of violence to defend myself against people in authority who abused their powers, ignored me and tried to silence me when I spoke out, which started over forty years ago.

I was in Coity Ward (known as Male A) which was downstairs and Ogmore Ward (Male B) was upstairs. Pen-y-fai had letters for male and female wards while across the road Glanrhyd had numbers.

I spent almost five months in Pen-y-fai hospital regularly being sedated with Valium and locked up in a cell without being listened to. I used to get worked up at the way I was being treated and not listened to and made threats to kill myself if I had to continue living like this. I started seeing a new child psychiatrist after being admitted to Pen-y-fai Hospital as Dr Hartley couldn't face me any more so I started seeing Dr K W Aron. She probably realised she had made a big mistake.

During my time in Pen-y-fai I was the youngest by at least six years. Other patients included Colin Afford, Steve Knight (from Tonna), Graham Pike, Lindsay Strachan, plus many more. One of the patients Cyril who had a house in the Sarn area painted his house trimmings in orange as he showed it me. Selwyn was a patient across the road in Glanrhyd and often stayed around the social centre. Another patient who lived in Pencoed by the old Esso Station close to the main railway line (London to Swansea) committed suicide. There were two Lillian's from Ffordd-yr-Eglwys in North Cornelly who were in Glanrhyd.

Some of the nurses were a bit cruel as well. It seems when someone is too sophisticated for them to exercise authority on they become aggressive - this wasn't discipline but abuse of authority and how people who are mentally weak behave to exercise power on vulnerable individuals. I was starting to become too much for anyone to control and ready to lash out at people. Several nurses I remember the name of, one being Chris Paget and another with a surname of Phelps. They were strict but the one who abused me I cannot remember his name as he was a young nurse. I was strong mentally and too much for any of them to get the better of me without abusing me.

This nurse was young with a scruffy mop of straw hair and loved to provoke me and get me worked up so he could inject Valium into my thigh and lock me up in a cell. He used to get great pleasure doing this because injecting Valium into my thigh gave me severe cramp in the muscle and he enjoyed seeing me suffer. It is quite likely that he did it for sexual pleasure (going by the pleasure he got injecting me and not any other way).

The only way I would calm down was when I was listened to and respected; but this didn't happen and so the sedation would only be temporary before I started lashing out again. The only way this would have stopped without repetitive sedation would be to put me to sleep (in other words kill me) which wouldn't have looked good, but I have reasons to believe that here and again later when I was being persecuted some people were trying to torment me to such an extent they were trying to make me commit suicide so that the truth of how I had been treated would never come out.

I was not prepared to tolerate being treated in the wrong for being different and blamed as if it was my fault for having epilepsy. I was also not going to be forced into silence or treated as guilty until proven innocent and expected to justify my innocence with others assuming the worse of me. As a result I had to resort to violence and destruction to get myself heard in an attempt to stop this persecution against me, if I had sat back and took it all my life would have been ruined, so I had to make myself unbearable for many in order to progress. Once provoked and my temper started up, I wouldn't give in and I drove many to tears and the point of despair – some even wishing they were dead. They upset me with their false allegations and negativity aimed at me, so if they had no consideration for me why should I care how they felt when I had to defend myself in this way? I didn't care if they were suicidal after I had finished with them.

Sometimes life was so unbearable I would threaten to kill myself if I ended up in trouble, was continued to be treated inappropriately or wasn't left alone. I sometimes started self-harming and smashing things up in rage or even tearing off my clothes (shirt/coat).

THE WORSE I WAS TREATED, THE WORSE I BEHAVED

Ever since the day when I went berserk, throughout the time I had epilepsy I have been a threat to people who inflict their evils of inferiority on me. Every incident of violence has been in defence against evils of inferiority being inflicted on me. Should anyone pose a risk to me like this and overstep their bounds by intruding into my freedom trying to control me I would go for them.

I was not a threat to people who treat me properly or at least reasonably – I was a risk to those who expect preferential treatment and treat me in the wrong if I don't sacrifice my freedom and rights for their preferences and demands because if they were to push me too far I would lose control of myself and give them what they deserved.

If ever others tried to control me and wouldn't leave me alone I would sometimes start throwing things about and tearing off my clothes. For a short time I carried a penknife with me and was prepared to slash my wrist if someone overstepped their bounds with trying to control me and deny me my freedom.

Isn't it strange how Bridgend became the suicide capital of the UK over thirty years later? Could there be some connection with experimentation, abuse and neglect of the families concerned by the authorities like how I was treated?

Whenever I couldn't survive by peaceful means I did whatever I could within my capabilities to protect myself and get justice or revenge where possible. JR (my initials) equals Justice or Revenge; and justice is a first choice, only revenge is used as a last resort if I cannot get justice.

Even today, I get provoked with blame, undermined because I don't do what others want, assumed the worst of and being treated as guilty until proven innocent knowing those doing it will never accept my innocence with them factuating their beliefs and ridiculing the truth.

v. Lingfield Hospital School, Surrey

In August 1973 I started at Lingfield Hospital School in Surrey which was for children with special needs who couldn't manage in mainstream school. For me this was a punishment as I could cope with mainstream school – if I wasn't being bullied and abused I would have remained well-behaved like I was described in my school report. It wasn't the best place for me as I was too advanced for both the pupils and the teachers there and I felt I was a prisoner and being punished for being too good. Why should I be locked up and institutionalised for being a victim of abuse is what I was thinking of and I became quite unruly within this school.

I was homesick and started running away on a regular basis. Although there were some very distressing times due to uncertainty of my future thinking I was going to be locked up for the rest of my life and threatening to kill myself because of the fear of being institutionalised for the rest of my life there was plenty of enjoyment and relief when I got my freedom and ran away.

The headmaster was Mr Thomas who was originally from Port Talbot and the deputy headmaster was Mr Evans who was originally from Neath.

Over the months I got to know the Surrey, Sussex and Kent countryside but became particularly familiar with the Lingfield, Blindly Heath, Edenbridge, East Grinstead, Crawley, Haywards Heath, Crowhurst, and then later Godstone, Oxted, Caterham and Purley areas as I used to head for London these ways.

Some of the areas I got to know quite well were the A22 up to Godstone then the Caterham by-pass. I sometimes went through Caterham but eventually got to Purley and South Croydon. There were many times I took the train to East Croydon and whenever I go that way now it brings back memories. Clapham Junction was another station I got off at regularly when running away as I tried to be as unpredictable as I could for the police. It is surprising how many of the roads around here have changed over the years.

The M23 and M25 were under construction with the M25 only being a little stretch either side of Godstone. I would sometimes watch from a bridge what was going on there.

I also liked pens and started taking my collection seriously as I needed a reliable pen to make notes of what was going on and record various happenings. I don't know where the notes went but my pen collection has grown quite significantly. The first two were purchased from Alders in Croydon and were Paper Mate Talisman ballpoint pen and propelling pencil which were bought separately. The ballpoint pen cost £2.95. My collection now exceeds 1,000 different pens.

The song "The Streak" by Ray Stevens came out and it prompted a lot of males to streak – I did a streak across the football pitch outside the building (Griffiths) I was resident in as a protest of not having my freedom.

In September and October 1974 I twice got the entire way home to Bridgend and sparked more concerns over my wellbeing. To get to Bridgend I needed £2.51. The single fares:

- From Lingfield to London Victoria was 33p
- From London Victoria to London Paddington (Underground) was 15p
- From London Paddington to Bridgend was £2.03.

I had a reserve of £2.51 to get all the way home if needed to.

With all the IRA bombings which had gone on I was told that with all the running away I was doing heading into London I might get killed by an IRA bomb. I said, "I would rather be killed by an IRA bomb than live like this".

Explosions around this time included:

10th September 1973	Kings Cross & Euston Stations
17th June 1974	IRA Bombs Parliament
17th July 1974	Tower of London Bomb Blast
5th October 1974	Guildford Pub Bombings
22nd October 1974	Bomb Blast in London Club
7th November 1974	Bomb Thrown into Woolwich Pub
21st November 1974	Birmingham Pub Bombings

After persistent reluctance to settle down, threatening to kill myself, causing unrest, making life very worrying and more escapes I finally got back into mainstream school. I had been living in fear of being institutionalised, denied my freedom and no proper education. I thought of killing myself if I was going to be imprisoned by the authorities for the rest of my life as I couldn't bear the thought of the evil and inferior holding me to ransom and preventing me from outperforming them – so the thought of suicide was a thought of freedom – away from all this.

During the first twenty-one months (March 1973 to December 1974) I contemplated suicide many times and was on the verge of committing it twice. On one occasion I had the intention of the equivalent of "pulling the trigger" (one more move and something would have happened) but my muscles wouldn't cooperate with my intentions so the final action didn't happen. It was like a numbing effect - I don't know if this was a defensive mechanism built into the brain when in dire straits to stop someone from doing something they would later regret. So it shows how desperate I was and if I hadn't tried it I wouldn't have known this would have happened.

I left the school in December 1974 with pneumonia.

I have visited the school at random on my own a few times and in 2007 and 2011 there were reunions organised by Phil Ford who I keep in touch with now.

When I visited the school in 2007 I saw a plaque on a building named after Lord Howe of Aberavon. It was strange that after Lingfield the next school which I started in January 1975 was in Aberavon.

5. Remaining School Days

In Christmas 1974 I got over pneumonia and was looking forward to freedom of some kind again.

i. St Joseph's, Aberavon, Port Talbot

In January 1975 I started at St Joseph's RC Comprehensive School in Aberavon which is part of Port Talbot and managed to settle down, but like earlier experiences there were some who were out to make me look at fault to cover their faults.

I settled into school and started becoming too advanced for the maths class I was in. My maths teacher Mr Brimfield was another one of those who couldn't do his maths properly and because I knocked his son off top place he didn't like me. He even told my mother at a PTA meeting that I would never get CSE in maths. I don't know how he could conclude that when I sailed to top of the class - it was a clear defamation of character out of spite.

My mother was so angry she saw the headmaster, and I was put into the top class the next day which I then sailed to top position again.

I had a few fights and scuffles with other pupils but there was no abuse, just defamation of character by that one teacher Mr Brimfield. If I had let Mr Brimfield take control I wouldn't have progressed with my maths ability. There was no way I looked as if I couldn't do maths as everyone else observed it. I was undermined because I didn't do things HIS way as well as having knocked his son off top position and he wasn't good enough as a maths teacher, so he was trying to undermine me – just like many charlatans in positions of authority have tried to do.

In 1976 we moved up to Kenfig Hill and a welfare officer visited to help us with moving costs. He noted down on my mother's files that I had epilepsy but didn't offer any help. This record in my mother's files should have helped me get an ex-gratia payment for all the years of benefit I was conned out of.

I am still friends with some of my old school mates who have seen a big difference in me, they are pleased for how I have progressed but disgusted at the long term problems I continued to have for years after I left the school. They all agree that in one way I didn't get help because I wasn't backward (and capable) and on the other side I didn't get opportunity because I was handicapped (and not capable).

ii. Music

Ever since my problems started in 1973 music was one of my greatest therapies which relaxed me a lot. I liked music earlier but it really got going in me (like my zest for freedom) and provided music for various events. I didn't have the equipment to be a DJ but had a big collection of music.

One particular song which I liked and was controversial at the youth club was Y Viva Espana by Sylvia. The girls loved it but the boys disliked it, so it was used as a closing song each week. Even today when I meet some of my school friends we have a laugh about it when we hear the song on our collections – it seems to jog our memories of dislike and winding others up when it is played as well as enjoyment.

The song "My Ding-A-Ling" by Chuck Berry was also a controversial song as those in charge would disapprove it.

Other favourites include: Monster Mash; See My Baby Jive; The Ballroom Blitz; Sugar Baby Love; Tiger Feet; Amoureuse; Forever & Ever to name but a few. Does anyone remember the instrumental song "Footsie" where an audience cheer with "Footsie"? This was an unusual tune but I liked it (and still do).

Music certainly helped me take my mind off some of the problems and to make up for the trauma I was going through I trained my mind to relax. This still takes place as when I hear any of the songs which were around then and I had trained to relax myself with I still get that relaxing feeling even though it isn't needed or as important now. Some songs would take me into another world (sort of) and today I feel as if I am floating away to some extent back into my fantasies. That is probably part of the reason why I am into music and although a baritone I sing either tenor or bass as required. My voice has also helped me in more ways than one.

iii. Summers of 1975 & 1976

These two summers played an important part in getting out and about since the summer of 1975 was the first summer of freedom (if you can call it that) and with the weather being so good I insisted to get out and about and this prepared me for coping on my own. Similarly for the summer of 1976 it was another bumper year and helped me get out and about rather than being stuck indoors with the rain.

It is amazing how much difference the weather can make – perhaps if we had two wet summers it could have impaired my adventuring – I don't know but it certainly lifted the feelings in these hard times.

iv. Fish & Chips

During my final years in school my love of fish and chips was starting to grow on me and I was known for it. Even today my preferred meal is fish and chips and I must have it at least four times a week. Matthew Jenkins opposite Pyle Library was my first well-liked chippie, then Gino's up the road and over the years I have been to many. Today I like Whelan's and Senior's nearby in Lytham, and Finnegan's and Beales fish & chip shops in the Bridgend/Porthcawl areas. Even today, I try to have a variety in what I eat but I cannot be taken away from fish and chips.

v. Back To Mynydd Cynffig Comprehensive School, Kenfig Hill

I left school in July 1977 as they didn't do the courses I wanted and re-joined Mynydd Cynffig Comprehensive School in September.

I started to enjoy a bit more freedom and got a pushbike for Christmas in 1977.

Unfortunately, earlier experiences of what it was like in this school tormented me and I couldn't settle down. Two teachers were rather inconsiderate as they took no account of my true abilities and what I had been through. I had mentioned some ideas I had in maths and they ridiculed me - yet later on I found out that my ideas were true so they again used the power of their position to treat me as wrong because they didn't want to recognise my ability. This is where conventional teaching doesn't recognise a potential genius and if it is not along the syllabus we are ridiculed by the teachers. If they understood what I was getting at they would have seen what I was thinking was a way forward for further ideas.

So this was a wasted year and I left in Easter 1978 and had to sign on. I enquired at Social Security about entitlements for care regarding my epilepsy. I was misled and only found out in 1993 I should have been getting disability benefits all the time.

So unemployment gave me a great opportunity for me to exercise my cycling skills and freedom to see how safe it was for me to go out and about on my own. I wasn't going to be restricted to the community and managed to do over 100 miles in a day on occasions. It was my only independent mode of transport and I used it to travel the valleys and neighbouring areas such that I knew my way round more than most people.

6. Conned By Social Security

i. Social Security, Crown Buildings, Angel Street, Bridgend

This was the next act which continued the impairment of my progress. had I been treated properly the problems I experienced during school days might have eventually passed by but due to being conned out of my entitlements when I was in more need of care and support than many it resulted in my health suffering and my studies being impaired as financial hardship caused more seizures and I couldn't afford what I needed for studying.

Thus after graduating it then gave The Manpower Services Commission and Social Services another opportunity to hold me to ransom yet further. You will see how Social Security didn't see me worthy of being entitled to disability benefits because of my capabilities whereas the manpower services commission saw me as not having the capabilities of an ordinary worker and treated me as subnormal. both these are part of the DWP now so one side of the department saw me as too capable for support whereas the other side saw me as not capable enough for opportunity.

ii. Trapped In A Black Hole

So I was trapped in a "black hole" where I wasn't disabled enough for support because of my intelligence; and in spite of being gifted I was treated as subnormal because of my disability – when I was both disabled and gifted. So this is direct contradiction where an irrelevant factor is used to devalue the qualifying criteria to deny me my rights.

There are many disadvantaged and vulnerable individuals who end up in black holes being neglected and left out of support.

These black holes are created by privileged cheats who have the same mentality as cowards from The Weakest Link and try to make the stronger look weaker because these cowards want to be seen as better and in order to maintain their false one-upmanship they have to do what they can to suppress the progress of many individuals who have greater potential than they have in order to stay on top. Many MPs fall into this category, and since many are lawyers it shows how they use the law to bend the rules for their preferences at the expense of the vulnerable.

So as well as the NHS causing me health problems for life the DWP has caused me financial and development problems for life too since the damage caused by poverty during my years of development and being labelled as subnormal has changed me from performing at an outstanding level before the problems started to an under performer but a fighter even though a lot of talent has gone to waste and been replaced by violence and destruction.

During the time I was unemployed during the spring and summer of 1978 I went to the Social Security Offices in Crown Buildings, Angel Street, Bridgend and enquired about my entitlements to disability benefits. There were two occasions I can remember asking - one being when I enquired about getting a travel permit to be looked after by relatives while my mother went into hospital as it was unsafe for me to live on my own unsupervised. I asked about the travel permit as well as entitlements to disability benefits and can clearly remember the mouthy worker at the desk trying to be a smart arse. She judged me like judging a book by its cover and her body language showed that she was being smug. She might have thought that she was clever, but her ignorance and inferiority had a devastating consequence on my personal development as I was subjected to many extra years of poverty and underperformance due to this hardship on top of my illness and the trauma I was going through.

I was so frustrated at having been treated like this I had a grand mal seizure on the way home and was rushed into hospital. While in hospital a travel permit was obtained without question for me to be looked after by relatives.

Due to the nature of the epilepsy being uncontrolled and putting my life at risk I should have had high level care and medium level mobility as I should have had an escort with me. But I was prepared to put my life at risk to get some freedom even though I was denied what I was entitled to.

But then the DWP is mostly for supporting the incompetent and the feckless, not people in genuine need of support.

I was beginning to feel that the gravities of status, authority and abuse of power by those responsible within the public sector were sucking me further into this black hole and if I didn't do something my life would be destroyed and recognition for my potential completely disappeared as others would always assume I was backward – like being treated as guilty until proven innocent and not given a fair chance to prove my potential.

As you will see later on, I tried to get backdated benefit for the money they had conned me out of as I had sufficient proof for an ex-gratia payment but they did all they could to invalidate my claim which was perfectly genuine and valid - they conveniently lost my notes to make my claim invalid because by the time they found my notes again it was past the validity time and so my case was no longer valid. Charlatans Alistair Darling and Ian McCartney in the early 2000's have tried to lay the blame on us saying the onus was on us to claim – even though we asked and were misled by corrupt civil servants.

Single mothers who have never worked or had a secure relationship to bring up their children who don't love their children but make a career living off the state got more support than my mother got, and later when she had to give up her career to care for me she got no additional support for doing what the state should have provided. So the authorities looked for every opportunity to betray and exploit us. I bet this was part and parcel of the plan to keep us suppressed so that the truth would never come out. Well it has now.

There is no doubt that I have been betrayed and abused by bureaucratic charlatans in positions of authority who have abused their position to undermine me. No matter what I try to do they always come out squeaky clean – but then they never honour the truth but only what works in their favour. Many vulnerable individuals who are already in severe hardship for a civilised nation are conned out of their entitlements while many fraudsters get loads of money as a luxury pretending it is for a disability.

7. Freedom With A Pushbike & By Bus & Train

i. Mind Over Matter

In 1978 when I had left school my freedom was more important than anything and I treasured it. I used the bike combined with mind over matter to get about as much as I could as well as save some money on bus fares so I could take my bike with me on a trip to another part of the UK by train and do more exploring. Most of the time I did this as a day away and being out and about on my own was a small risk but there would always be someone ready to call the emergency services if necessary.

Cycling did a lot for me as it helped get the frustrations out of my system and build me into being stronger, together with learning about the risks I was taking given the circumstances I would be in. there were times I was in some potentially dangerous situations should I have gone into a seizure but I took all the precautions I could to ensure I was safe should one happen.

So, freedom which I had been denied during my childhood meant so much to me such that over the years I got around more of England and Wales using my bike and public transport than most people did with a car. I had visited every city and most major towns in England and Wales unescorted and most with my bike while I had uncontrolled epilepsy. It shows I wasn't going to be a prisoner within society trapped within my locality and I was prepared to take chances and carried out the necessary precautions to minimise the risk of danger to me (and others).

One good thing for 99% of the time while I wasn't under the influence of an epileptic seizure nobody could tell I had the condition and I was treated more normally than where I lived since there was some prejudice against me by people who knew I had the condition. Obviously if I had a seizure then others would know, but when it didn't happen I was treated better generally. It was great to get out and about and find my way, and later after brain surgery I started driving and get around the UK as much as I can.

In the late 1970s and early 1980s one of my most frequent visits was to the Midlands where I would travel there and back in a day by train. In those days, British Rail issued what was called an Awayday ticket. It was a day return and I used to find the Awayday tickets excellent value for money. Sometimes I would stay with relatives and tour the region I was staying in. I would also visit the New Forest area and go between Weymouth and Portsmouth. Sometimes I would take a train to London for the day.

Whenever I visited London, if I had the time I would often retrace the escape routes I travelled when escaping from Lingfield Hospital School. I can do that much easier now with a car, but I would often go to East Croydon and retrace what I could as well as visit Alders. If time permitted I would go to Caterham and other places I escaped to including Godstone, Oxted and more. I would even take my bike but that was normally when I avoided the train by London. I don't think I would have been allowed to take my bike on the underground.

Generally I would travel anywhere from The Midlands to The South Coast, so all of Southern England and Wales were within easy reach of a day out and occasionally I would venture out further north.

Most of my northern travels were when I took a holiday in Blackpool. I would get a Regional Rail Rover and travel all over the North West with a few extra extensions of journey to places like Newcastle, Durham, Whitby, Hull, York, etc. In September 1988 I visited Lockerbie as this was the furthest extent of the ticket and had never heard of it before – but a few months later everyone knew of it because of the Pan Am bombing over the town. In 1990 I had already done so much travelling around in the north of England I decided to get a Seven Day All-Line Rail Rover – and because I wanted to treat myself I got it First Class as this is the only Rail Rover you can get first Class. So I had a treat and an incident with three yuppies which is mentioned further down.

However, there were a few incidents when I had a seizure which was a bit embarrassing but funny now. One I clearly remember was at a shopping centre in Watford at around the mid to late 1980s.

I was looking around a shopping centre in Watford when I started having a seizure. There was a bed shop and the bed nearest the entrance looked a bit like mine at home. When I came out of the seizure and was confused a bit, I saw what I thought was my bed and did what you can expect. I stripped down to my underpants to have a lie down and a rest after the seizure, only to find out as I recovered more I was in the middle of a shopping centre.

Some people who looked on must have wondered what sort of a nutcase I must be, but those dealing with me understood and were quite good about it. I was most apologetic and embarrassed at the time but it couldn't have been helped as it was my instinct to get to bed after a seizure and rest.

There have been numerous incidents where I have had a seizure and some confusion has broken out but most realise what was happening and have been very helpful. These experiences certainly let me see the nicer caring side of society and I got to know a few people who cared for me after a seizure. One I can remember who helped me at a shopping centre was David Green (or Dave Green I think he was known as). This happened around 1994/95 and he was very helpful and considerate. I wish there were more like him.

However there were many incidents where trouble broke out. These took place during and after I had epilepsy up to about 1999. Bus drivers tried to be smart and claim I wasn't disabled as if I was trying to get concessionary travel when I shouldn't. Well one driver got his comeuppance with a load of mayhem. Most of these incidents happened when I had epilepsy – nowadays I try to avoid conflict as I don't use the public transport as much and I am normally travelling when it is less busy.

i. Concessionary Troubles

I had a disabled person's concessionary bus pass and could use it at any time. When living in the Bridgend area which came under National Welsh they only issued tickets with Child, Adult and OAP on. There was nothing with Concessionary or Disabled, so whenever I got a ticket it had

OAP on it.

One day in the late 1980s I got a Roverbus ticket to travel to the Swansea area which comes under South Wales Transport. I got onto a local bus in Swansea at the Quadrant Centre showing my concessionary pass and my Roverbus ticket, but the driver refused to let me on. He argued I got the ticket off a senior citizen but I tried to explain this is what disabled people have. He was stubborn and wouldn't accept or check this was the case and even queried what I was doing with a disabled pass since in those days you had to be physically disabled or the disability had to be visible to be accepted as disabled and with me being fit and healthy it was hard to convince the driver this was the case. He was trying to be a smartarse and make me look small so I was starting to get rather worked up.

An argument broke out and I tried to be assertive as I was sick of being undermined, made out to be a liar and suffering for others faults, so I was getting rather worked up. I could sense a seizure coming on and it turned out to be the onset of a grand mal since the anger and rage had intensified the situation and this was one of the worse seizures I had in many years.

All of a sudden I collapsed into unconsciousness and was sick, I soiled my pants and there was panic and mayhem. The service was abandoned, but while all passengers were innocent and regret the inconvenience and experience they had, I felt there could be no shying away from the truth for the driver that I was disabled and entitled to use a concessionary pass in spite of looking fit and healthy.

This must have been one of the most disturbing experiences this bus driver had after trying to tread on me like dirt. I hate stubborn individuals like him who see the worst in me and refuse to accept the truth. I have no regrets for the psychological effects this has had on him.

ii. Bus Company Doesn't Care

At around the same time, National Welsh which was based in Cardiff operated a commuter service from Bridgend to Cardiff and I was told by head office that I could use my weekly season ticket on this service if there were seats available; however if seats were reserved by others they had priority. So on numerous occasions I tried to use my ticket on this service but bus drivers said I could come on if I was to buy a ticket. This meant there were seats available and I showed the drivers the letter, but they refused to let me on without paying an extra fare. I complained to head office of National Welsh but they never sorted the problem out. This is yet another act where those with inferior capabilities want to come out on top and invert the truth making innocent individuals look in the wrong. Life was so depressing in the Bridgend area with stubborn and pretentious wrongdoers not honouring the truth or doing what they should.

iii. Queue Barging

Another day in the late 1980s I was waiting for a bus in Bridgend and was the first passenger waiting for the next bus. A queue was forming and I had a seizure.

During the time I had the seizure and was recovering the bus driver arrived, all the other passengers got on and I recovered just in time to board the bus before it left and I was the only passenger left standing - yet I was first in the queue and needed a seat the most as I was unsteady and recovering from a seizure. I asked if I could have a seat as I was first in the queue but did anyone give me a seat I was entitled to? No.

I was referred to as a drug addict and other unpleasant things and provoked by another passenger as well as told to wait my turn and he mocked me. When he got off I got off too and gave him his just deserves.

iv. Three Yuppies In First Class

An act of revenge in a peaceful way which has been the best story I have told regarding three yuppies on a train. This happened in 1990 in the midst of all the suffering so there were some good times too - especially when I was away from the oppression I was experiencing most of the time. It was the most peaceful and effective act of revenge I have ever had - especially as it was against some elitist yuppies

I was travelling on a London Victoria to Brighton train where the yuppies thought I didn't have a First Class ticket because I was casually dressed in jeans and had a carrier bag - not dressed in a pin-striped suit with an executive case.

The first yuppie said to me, "Excuse me sir, this is First Class", to which I looked at the window and replied, "Oh yes, so it is".

The second yuppie then said to me, "You need a First Class ticket to travel in here, so please leave", to which I replied, "It doesn't matter what ticket I have as long as the inspector doesn't come to check the tickets. Anyway there were no other seats and this is a spare seat so this will do".

The third yuppie then said, "You shouldn't be I here, so please leave", to which I replied, "Excuse me but you have no authority over me. You are a passenger, just like me and I have a right to a seat just like you have, so I am staying put".

The looks of disgust on their faces made me wonder what next I was in line for. Perhaps they were going to report me or I just had to wait.

After about five minutes after departure from London Victoria we could hear the inspector in the background. I started fidgeting with my fingers and looking worried and I could see the three yuppies making eye-to-eye contact with each other as if to be saying, "He's going to be in trouble, we'll have the last laugh". I wanted to wind them up so much that when the truth came out it was a huge disappointment.

When the inspector came and checked the tickets he was more polite to me than them as they had daily or return tickets - each yuppie had their ticket clipped and he said "Thanks" to each of them, but all he did with me was glance at my ticket and then said, "Thank you very much sir" and smiled at me. He was probably surprised and thought he had better treat me with more respect.

When the inspector left I looked over and said to the yuppies, "Well, have you anything to say now?" They sulked and avoided eye-to-eye contact with me for the remainder of the journey and when we all got off I told them it was nice travelling First Class and one of the best journeys I have had and wished them all the best.

I would like to have known what was going through their minds.

v. Misleading Signs

Sometime around about May 1993 I was exploring and had planned on getting the last train from Stockport to Blackpool. The platform for the Blackpool train was 3a but there was no clear sign for 3a being a dead end cutting between platforms 3 and 4. In fact by the main entrance and the stairs all the signs had were Platform 3 and Platform 4.

Unfortunately I missed the last train as I had been waiting on Platform 3 down by the 3a end but it wasn't clear. In other stations where a platform is separate there are signs but in Stockport there wasn't.

I had to get a taxi home which cost £55 so the next day I went to Stockport again with a camera to take pictures for evidence.

I them compiled a letter requesting a refund due to inadequate information misleading me but got nowhere. They tried to wrangle their way out of it claiming signs were adequate but I had evidence they weren't when I took the photos and this helped me get past their lies.

I had to go through various channels and put in an application via the Small Claims Court for a refund. A hearing was due in London which I was prepared to attend but days before this I received a letter from British Rail (Macmillan House, Paddington) for an out of court settlement for all expenses which totalled £148.50 instead of just £55 which I accepted.

Persistence worked but it took over a year.

vi. Punch-Up At Euston

In September 1993 I was catching the last train of the day from Euston to Preston and was waiting to be served at John Menzies at the station.

Along comes a commuter who pushes into the front of the queue and shoves me out of the way as I am about to be served. If he had been a bit more polite I wouldn't have thought any more of it but being treated his way made me whack him one in the face and a punch up broke out.

This was reported to the British Transport Police and the train I was due to get on was delayed by about three quarters of an hour while they took statements.

After all the questioning took place I was escorted onto the train by the police and passengers were making remarks at me pointing the finger at me again.

I made it clear that I was the victim and if they keep picking on me I will bring the train to a stop again by giving someone a taste of their own medicine for picking on me and I will argue I was the victim again. After that everyone left me alone worried they might be attacked if they said anything to me. I was ready to let anyone who picked on me have it.

vii. Miserable Old Cows

In 1994 an incident was when I was travelling to The Midlands by train to see the family (which I no longer have anything to do with now). I had to change trains at Crewe and got a train to Birmingham New Street. It was rather busy and many seats were reserved, so I looked for one which was free for my stretch of journey and I came across one so sat in it.

The journey went peaceful until we got to Wolverhampton where a woman got on, looked at the seats and accused me of occupying her seat. She showed me the reservation ticket she had in her hand and instructed me to get out of her seat - no manners at all.

The ticket on the seat didn't agree but she was pompous and condescending and I argued with her about what it said on the seat. She was getting mouthy with me and thinking British Rail had made a mistake I gave her the benefit of the doubt and the seat based on the so-called evidence she provided me with which I late found out to be invalid.

I was angry and decided to note down the details to make a complaint to British Rail and in doing so noticed that the direction of the train didn't reflect the direction on the reservation. This is because the train started out one way and turned at a station so forward was backward and vice versa, so I told the lady that the seat facing her (which was occupied by another lady of her type) was in her seat and asked if I could have my seat back but she refused.

I told her that she was so keen to have her seat so now ask that woman in her reserved seat to get out of the way so I can have my seat back. She started to slag me off again and I got so angry I told her she had got a seat under false pretences and that seat was not reserved so could I have my seat back but she refused. So I decided to let her know what I thought of her and let everyone in the carriage know. I said it out aloud and everyone in the carriage must have heard me yell, "You are a miserable old cow getting a seat under false pretences and treating me a young male with contempt".

The lady opposite then joined forces with her and treated me in the wrong so a bit of a fracas broke out and the inspector was called for. I explained that she has obtained a seat under false pretences and when he looked at her reservation and the ticket on the seat he told her that her seat facing her which was the seat the other lady was occupying and the seat she was in which I was in before was not reserved along this stretch. The inspector confirmed I was in the right and that the other lady facing her was occupying her seat. The train had turned en route and forward was back and backward was forward.

So when the inspector left I asked her if I could have my seat back but she stubbornly refused so I taunted them until I got to my destination calling them man haters and let the two ladies in tears. As I got off a man interfered and hit me across the head which I returned a punch to his face and left him shocked.

I was wholly innocent and was not prepared to be denied what was rightfully mine so this is what I had to resort to in order to defend myself and get revenge on those who cheat their way out of mistakes and treating me in the wrong when I was completely innocent.

I try to sort things out peacefully but sometimes the other side gets a bit too pushy and aggressive and start to go beyond what they should. Once they have degraded me to the lowest of the low my temper and emotions are quick to go out of control and this is when disruption breaks out.

viii. Fare Dodger Tries To Point Finger At Me

In 1995 I was travelling south and the inspector had been to check all tickets. I was in a smoking carriage as there were no seats available in the non-smoking carriage so I was watching to change seats if the opportunity was there.

Part of the way down inspectors changed and the new inspector hurried unusually through the carriage.

At the next station a lot of passengers got off from down the non-smoking area so I decided to move seats and sat in the non-smoking carriage. I moved at the same time other passengers were getting on.

There was one passenger with an unusual look in his eye looking over at me but I can only remember thinking what's up with him. A but later the new inspector came asking to see tickets from the last station. Having already been on the train and had my ticket inspected it didn't apply to me but this guy saw it as an opportunity to be clever and pointed me out as having just got on the train.

I made it clear that I hadn't just got on but changed seats to sit in the non-smoking carriage. I also mentioned that I saw the inspector hurrying with a bag in his hand which was unusual, so doesn't that prove I was already on the train?

The inspector agreed but in order to fulfil his duty he still asked to see my ticket again. I queried why he wanted to see my ticket having proven I had already been on the train and my gut feeling was to get this guy's tickets checked as I had a feeling he was a fare dodger. So I said to the inspector I will willingly show you my ticket as long as you check his ticket as he has caused this and there are no exceptions, otherwise I will refuse to show you my ticket on the grounds of prejudice since there is a difference between checking tickets on demand and being induced by someone misleading you and treating me as guilty until proven innocent.

The inspector asked him for his ticket but guess what? He didn't have a valid ticket and looked for excuses to get out of showing his ticked (which he hadn't got). After he was issued with a penalty fare or whatever it was I showed my ticket and proved my innocence.

Some people will try to make others look in the wrong if it increases their chances of getting away with wrongdoing. Such people I refer to as opportunist wrongdoers. Well it backfired on him and I had the last laugh.

ix. Bossy Old Cow Against Young Male

In 1995 I got on a bus and sat in the front seat which was reserved for concessionary and disabled passengers. The front seat on the other side was occupied by two teenage girls.

At one bus stop an obnoxious but physically fit female pensioner got on and looked at me stubbornly. I could see she disapproved of me sitting where I was and after making no move she challenged me for sitting there. I told her I was within my rights to sit there and she had no right to question me and to mind her own business. She tried to intimidate me so I made reference to the teenage girls sitting on the other front seat and asked her why she had a go at me. I suggested she would rather have a go at a middle-aged male than young girls because I am a male so it is all right for teenage girls to occupy the disabled/elderly seat but not me and referred to her as a man hater.

I didn't get out of the way for her but as I was so angry I decided to get off at the same stop she got off at to frighten her. I didn't follow her after I got off but felt she deserved to be taught a lesson for picking on me.

x. Cycle Traps

One day around 1997 I decided to use my bike and locked it against some railings near the corner of a car park. While I was away someone with a mobility scooter had left it right up against the corner and someone else had parked their car alongside the scooter and my bike.

When I went to fetch my bike I saw what had happened and a grumpy degrading man accused me of "blocking him in" and being inconsiderate when locking my bike up. He hurled a lot of abuse at me with false allegations. I did nothing wrong as neither of these two vehicles were there when I when I locked my bike up, so as I hadn't started unlocking my bike I decided to leave it there and walked away leaving the guy's scooter trapped. This was in response to how he wrongfully accused me of causing the problem, so that is what I eventually did – caused him a problem for wrongful accusations.

I didn't want to return while he was there so I waited until he had gone. Later that evening I saw they were both still there and also the following morning. However, during the day I noticed they had both gone so I then unlocked my bike and left.

I don't care how much inconvenience I caused this guy who couldn't get his mobility scooter after all the false allegations and blame aimed at me. He shouldn't have been so silly to have put it in the corner and the driver of the car parked alongside should have been more considerate. None of it was my fault, so he got what he deserved for blaming and being nasty towards someone who was innocent.

xi. Reserved Injustice

In 1998 I was travelling north and the train company announced that the seat reservation system had failed and so no reservations can be honoured for this train's service. So with no reservation in force and the train getting rather full I had to get a seat in a crowded area.

About half way along the journey someone got on with a ticket reserved for the seat I was sitting in - and guess what? A fight eventually broke out.

It was announced that no reservations were valid but this passenger insisted he had proof this was his seat and I should get out. I made it clear that if the seat reservation was working I would have seen this was reserved and got another seat so since it isn't working it is he it has failed, not me and I made it clear that it had been announced that no reservations were valid so he should claim a refund for not having his seat reserved.

He didn't like this and became aggressive towards me and a fight broke out. He started on me so I laid into him.

xii. Smoker Gets Puffed Up

Around Christmas in 1998 I was travelling from Blackpool North on a train in a non-smokers carriage and a female lit up a cigarette. I asked if she would put it out but her partner became rather stroppy with me and said that if I don't want the smoke I should move out. I told him if his partner wants to smoke she should smoke where it was permitted. Another passenger backed me up and asked her to put out her cigarette and she started playing up and broke into tears. Her partner got so angry he lashed out at the two of us and a fight broke out.

I dialled 999 explaining that a nutcase was lashing out. Various passengers witnessed this and he was arrested and escorted off the train at Preston station.

Several passengers who were witnesses were prepared to give statements but when I asked the police about how it was proceeding with being assaulted by him I found out that he had carried false identity and given a false address. It is believed he was from the Wolverhampton area. So it didn't go any further.

These examples of what happened are there not for pity, sympathy or boasting about, but to demonstrate how someone who is generally so peaceful who respects others and will go out of my way to help others can turn so disruptive which is a syndrome of years of abuse, betrayal and unfairness. The more exploitation of my goodwill I experience the quicker I withdraw my goodwill whereas the happier I am the more goodwill I will deliver.

I have no regrets for these and many other disturbances I have been involved in where defending myself from the evils of inferiority and selfishness of others trying to use me as a stepping stone for their advantage and treating me as if I was worthy of dirt or didn't know the difference between right and wrong.

8. University Hospital, Cardiff

Since 1975 I was to attend this hospital trying to get my epilepsy under control. There were mentions of brain surgery but nothing ever progressed - maybe it was just to make them look as if they were trying but I think they wanted to experiment with me on various drugs including the anticonvulsant drug Epilim.

i. Epilim

Like with other medication I tried Epilim in all goodwill but I can clearly remember not feeling too good after I started taking it and so after about two or three weeks this was around 1980 and I decided to come off it and refused to take any more. It made me feel worse so I wasn't going to take it anymore. It was a good job since the drug has caused many problems for people who have been prescribed it.

ii. Other Drug Problems

The only other drug I refused to take was Lamotragine which I was prescribed in the late 80s or early 90s which gave me blurred vision a few hours after taking it. I would take it at breakfast time and by the time I was in work the effects were felt.

iii. Many Other Drugs

I was also being tried on all different drugs to get my epilepsy under control and for a long time was on the maximum dose of anticonvulsants which could be prescribed to a patient. They had a significant doping effect on my brain power but even on all this I was still quite sharp and more alert than the average person. My IQ was still in the super-gifted zone when I was on all this medication.

9. Student Days - College & University

Throughout my student days I got an annual grant which helped a little but there was no weekly allowance for being a student from a family with low income so this in addition to my medical condition and being conned out of disability benefits impaired my personal development. My mother had to subsidise my education from her paltry income and I had to take part time work at weekends and during holidays. Sometimes I needed to cycle 20 miles each way to attend college in order to save money.

i. Swansea College Of Further Education

In September 1978 I enrolled at Swansea College of further Education in Tycoch and did pretty well there over the two years. The college was about 18 miles each way and I had to commute every day for my studying.

I was starting to enjoy a bit more freedom and had the urge to go further, so what I would do was try to save some money I would have spent on bus fares by cycling to and from college and when I had saved enough up I would have a day away on the train setting off early on a Saturday morning to get somewhere by lunchtime, have all day cycling around and then back home by midnight. I couldn't stay overnight anywhere so had to get back home every day.

Cycling to college wasn't too much but there were times when I have had a seizure close to the day coming to a close at 16:00 and all knowing I had my bike. I told them to let me get my energy back and I would be able to cycle home - which I did. I was normally on the bike within half an hour of a seizure and made it all the way home.

As I was thinking of going to university, Josephine my mother's half-sister or my step aunt was one who couldn't accept me for what I was and tried to convince me that I should not go to university. She used excuses like, "Your mother is struggling to make ends meet, and so you should get a job, not be a student or go to university". She was never particularly bright but tried to be clever and in doing so had to bring others down. When I started at university she didn't want to have anything to do with me again. Over the years she has alienated other members of her family and is something of a loner. She is typical of a dictatorial cheat.

I sat my A-levels but one question in the Applied Maths I misinterpreted and did a lot more than was necessary and demonstrated my maths beyond A-level, but in spite of this it cost me a grade and was the only grade B I got. Not getting Grade A for all was a blow.

Since then I have never had faith in exams because misinterpretation due to poorly worded questions (which broad-minded individuals can see) leading us astray and we get penalised for demonstrating additional abilities when we put our imagination to use. Demonstrating ability beyond those at the top or in charge results in punishment so I would rather avoid being tested. I have done whatever I can to avoid exams and tests and didn't sit my finals.

I am happy to be seen as bottom-of-the-class in spite of having more of a connection with genius than those who got Grade A.

ii. A Phobia Of Exams And Tests

This started a phobia against exams and I have never had trust in exams or test since we are subjected too much to the straight and narrow and if we demonstrate our abilities and go another way we are penalised.

When it came to my finals in 1984 the phobia took over and I was too ill to sit them so ended up with an aegrotat degree. Also around 1990 when I was recommended for a MENSA test, I became ill again and although I tried it unattended when I wasn't worked up I couldn't commit to a prearranged test as I would become ill so I didn't join MENSA as it wouldn't accept the proof on medical grounds.

Whenever I can avoid tests or examinations I will since I hate them. They support the parrot fashioned and spoon-fed but penalise those of us who use our imagination and come up with our own methods. There are no exams for what you think up yourself because only you know it, thus you don't get recognised for your achievements you have thought up yourself.

iii. University Of East Anglia (UEA), Norwich

So, after getting my A-levels I started at the University of East Anglia but this wasn't ideal because of a number of factors. It wasn't cheap living away and having no financial support off my mother nor were my entitlements off the state I couldn't afford what I needed like the other students, and several students rather cruel to me. Some of the more pretentious and rough were rather nasty to me and penalised me for having seizures.

One day I was doing my washing up and had a seizure so didn't empty the sink. One of the students poured the water over my clothes as a form of punishment for not emptying the sink. There was no thought for what I was going through since a handful of students would use whatever they could to make times harder for me. If I had a seizure they would leave me in the gutter. The students that did this to me were the pretentious and nasty - false one-upmanship types who used the epilepsy to bring me down - I must have been too good for them and they were envious.

I didn't get on with these students who were bullies, so I ventured out a bit on my own. I would travel a lot by train and could get an Anglia Day Ranger ticket for £4 or a weekly ticket for £10. I went all over East Anglia visiting places from King's Lynn, Cromer, Great Yarmouth, Ipswich, Newmarket, Cambridge, Ely plus the many smaller places in between.

There were a few occasions when I asked a bit more about the maths and tried to get an explanation but was told, "That is beyond the scope of this course" to which it had a devastating effect on me since it stopped me from progressing naturally.

I lost interest in my studying because I couldn't get the information I needed felt rejected and circumstances (seizures, poverty and attitudes) made it uncomfortable for me.

The less capable students with spoon-fed privileges were overtaking me and picking on me. It was obvious form their tactics they were like cowards on The Weakest Link ganging up on someone who was too good so they must have been envious of me somehow to have treated me so badly. These external influences which I had no control over were inverting the truth against me so it wasn't worth me trying in an unfair and restricted environment, so I transferred to University College in Cardiff.

iv. University College, Cardiff

This was like in Swansea where I would commute but I was beginning to feel demoralised because of financial hardship and having more seizures. When the exams came round in 1984 I had frequent seizures and so couldn't sit my finals so all I was awarded was an aegrotat degree.

It was still a degree in Pure Maths, Applied Maths & Astronomy but the grade was not a reflection of my true mathematical capabilities. I never performed well in exams because I would have had more seizures than normal in the run-up to the exam and this drained me so I was never at my best. As a result I don't like exams because they don't give a true reflection of my abilities.

I didn't go to the awards ceremony to get my degree in cap and gown so I had it posted to me. I didn't want to look like I was standing on a pedestal in a cap and gown so refused.

I don't use the letters after my name since there are so many charlatans who have hollow, inflated or diluted capabilities that have letters after their name but they would never have got there if they weren't spoon-fed. They are a reflection of the spoon-feeding and having plenty handed to them on a plate. So if recognition can only be granted along selected lines where people are given the opportunity to do well and not just down to natural capabilities which is an insult to the disadvantaged since it hypes up the privileged then I don't recognise their qualifications. I recognise myself as having a connection with genius based on facts and not snobbery, which is more than any Oxford, Cambridge or any other elitist organisation can offer. There are some exceptional ones here but that is them, not the elitist institutions. So it looks like the truth of my capabilities will never be recognised by cheats will it? I reject them because they are false; anyone who rejects me does so because I am too good for them.

10. Early Career - Sheltered Placement Scheme

This was the biggest insult to my intelligence being treated as if I had less intelligence and potential than those with minimal qualifications doing basic administration work in an office when I had a degree in maths and an IQ of over 150. After graduating in 1984 I tried to get a job but everywhere refused to even consider me for a job. I had made more enquiries about disability benefits again but told I wasn't entitled to anything so I lived on unemployment benefit while seeking employment. After a year I was getting threats from Social Security that my benefit would be stopped if I didn't actively seek employment which I was doing.

Everyone who restricts the progress of someone must have a feeling of inadequacy or envy to need to bring someone down or restrict their progress like they did to me. I believe I must have been too good for them to have been treated like this as well as them being perverted to add insult to injury and they had to look for excuses to treat me with "Cowards of The Weakest Link" syndrome - this is where they gang up and abuse their authority to make the strongest look the weakest and destroyed my future for me (or tried to). They probably thought that once they got a hold of me I would never get away and progress, so this was their plan to keep me restricted as well as continually treated as guilty until proven innocent, which in the long term would prevent the truth from coming out. Well it might have worked temporarily but the truth has finally come out about what all these control freaks with perverted minds in power did.

Many adults who haven't got the numeracy skills of junior school children were recognised as more capable than me, so it shows it was a label to hinder my progress by control freaks with mentalities like cowards on The Weakest Link.

At the other end the fat cats argue that in order to get them to use their skills they have to be paid the going rate for their expertise which is nothing more than greed and exploitation holding employers to ransom. Then why was I held to ransom with my career and expected to deliver my talent and expertise for less than what some workers with basic CSE qualifications are getting?

Greed is inferiority as well as a quantity much used to substitute fake qualities in order to exercise false one-upmanship.

i. Mid Glamorgan Social Services Department

All of a sudden I got information that I had to go on what was then called The Sheltered Placement Scheme which was a scheme for disabled individuals who haven't got the ability to do a basic job and would be unemployable otherwise. It was in conjunction between Mid Glamorgan Social Services Department (MGSSD) and the then Manpower Services commission which is now a part of the DWP. I was forced onto it and if I didn't accept it I would lose my unemployment benefit and have nothing to live on as I wasn't getting any disability benefits which I was entitled to either.

I was also told that it would be a trial and if I could prove myself I would be taken off it and put into normal employment. Instead I was kept on it all the time and if I hadn't broken away from it by going into self-employment I might still have been on it today as I wouldn't have been able to prove my potential. Isn't it strange how I outperformed many and was kept on the scheme? They were all colluding to hinder me in order to hide the oppression I had been and was still going through.

In effect I was labelled as subnormal and was the only one in the entire authority on it – so I was on a lower tier of capability below everyone else and have a link with mathematical genius and a degree in maths treated as the least capable of workers in the entire authority. This shows the rot at the top where the strongest is made look the weakest by charlatans in positions of authority.

Isn't it strange how one part of the DWP (Social Security) saw me as not qualifying for disability benefits because I had capabilities and was too capable and the other side (Jobcentre/Manpower Services Commission) saw me as not capable enough to do a basic job?

This is typical of a corrupt government departments run by cheats and crooks for the benefits of cheats and crooks.

During this time on the scheme I was seeking other employment as I was fed up of being treated worse than school levers with GCSEs. I tried as much as I could to get away as I was most unhappy, occasionally suicidal and would take my frustrations out on the house when I got home.

On one occasion, Paddy Pope, my boss wanted me to go out to an office in Merthyr Tydfil to sort out some computer problems – funny how I was suddenly seen as capable when they wanted me to sort something out for them. Since I had been travelling by bus to and from work I didn't have my Disabled Persons Railcard with me but needed to go by train to Merthyr Tydfil. When I put in for travel expenses Paddy Pope refused to let me have a full refund and would only refund the disabled rate telling me it was my fault for not carrying it around with me. He didn't tell me I would need it and as it hadn't been issued by MGSSD it was their duty to refund my expenses. Paddy Pope was a typical smartarse who tried to make me suffer in whatever way he could. He wouldn't let me progress and every time he tried to be clever like this I was becoming more suicidal in work.

Paddy Pope (my boss at the time) said that being on The Sheltered Placement Scheme meant I was less capable than everyone else, so I started telling him what to do. He told me that I didn't have the authority to tell him what to do so I told him he didn't have the intelligence to undermine my intelligence. If he were to use his authority to insult my intelligence then I will use my intelligence to undermine his authority and told him what I thought of him.

Some days I would get picked on and not listened to which made me moody on the way home. During commute some commuters would be pushy and try to shove me about which didn't go down too well when I was already worked up and on several occasions minor punch ups broke out. I would get home frustrated and if anything went wrong I would start smashing up items in the house as well as breaking up the furniture - it was all a desperate attempt to get the message over that life wasn't worth living when I was continually being treated like an outcast with no abilities and subjected to persistent oppression.

ii. More Social Security Corruption

When I started this degrading job in 1985 I came off unemployment benefit and enquired about getting Supplementary Benefit until my first pay packet came through but I was refused. This was at Crown Buildings, Angel Street, Bridgend again and so they conned me out of a months' entitlement as well. When I found out I should have been getting it and enquired, I was given the smart-arsed answer "You managed to get by without it so you mustn't have needed it". It is not a matter of surviving on nothing but getting what I was entitled to. Does this mean I am expected to live on nothing? What a load of back street brains they have there.

iii. Why Couldn't I Get A Better Job

MGSSD was trying to lead me into believing I would never get another job because I wasn't good enough. This seemed strange as so often I would get shortlisted, sit an aptitude test and be selected for interview, but once a reference was asked for I never got any further. It was only where MGSSD had its say that my chances of progressing were ruined – like how cowards on The Weakest Link vote the strongest off as the weakest.

If I was such rubbish, why did they want to keep hold of me and stop me from progressing? Two possibilities here; firstly they were envious of me so didn't want me to progress; secondly it could have been a conspiracy with other authorities to keep me suppressed so that the truth of how I was treated earlier on in life would never got out. Why did they have to restrict my progress? The answer must be that I was a threat to their perverted and wicked ways.

I became suspicious and decided to scheme up with someone and pretend to go for an interview so that he could request a reference from MGSSD and forward it onto me and I could then see what they were saying about me.

My suspicions were true - they emphasised my so-called inability due to epilepsy which was false since epilepsy doesn't cause any inability but gave no credit to what I did beyond what I was paid to do. I was exploited for my talents and paid pittance so when I found out what had been said about me I took this matter up. I was accused of subterfuge but I had to do this to uncover the lies and control they had over my progress.

They thought that by giving insulting references which amounted to defamation of character they would have me "held" for my working life as nobody else would have me – and this was probably to suppress both the truth of how I was treated when I was younger as well as how they were treating me then. They feared that if I started to make progress then the truth would come out – which it has.

There were also many times when I was assumed to be at fault and was treated as guilty until proven innocent - which when I was innocent (every time) it means being treated inappropriately and below what I deserved. This had an effect on making me answer my boss back, using foul language and refusing to cooperate.

iv. The Midget With The Mighty Mouth

One colleague (my immediate boss) known as 3M because he was the Midget with the Mighty Mouth was always having a go at me and trying to promote his ego and he was rather short. He was a manipulative and sneaky person who would spy on me because he didn't want me to progress beyond him so he would try to keep one step ahead of me and catch me out where possible.

So one day I was getting rather fed up with his tactics and taunting so I set up a file on the computer I was using. It was in the days of DOS when we didn't have accounts and like this book I did an outline of him describing him something like "A midget with a brain the size of a pea and his mouth in the wrong place since what comes out is diarrhoea. He is vain and conceited so one day he will meet his match and be put into place..." The file also had some macro within it to record the time and date anyone viewed it. So I went to lunch and expected him to start his sneaky ways again.

When I got back from lunch I could see something of an unusual look in 3M's face and so I smiled at him. Thinking he had viewed the insults I was ready to wind him up even more. I looked at the file and it confirmed he looked at it within minutes of me leaving for lunch - shows how hasty he was. So I repeatedly smiled at him when I saw him and could see the scowl in his face.

He had two choices:

- Keep quiet about what he saw on the file and suffer in silence; or
- Speak out but admit to snooping on my work

So either way he would fall into the trap.

He kept quiet for a day or two but couldn't bottle it up so he engineered an excuse to report me to my manager for what I did. He claimed to have accidentally come across it and thought he had better report what I had put.

I told my boss that it was a set up to see if he was snooping on me and if he did (which he has now proven by indirect admission) I have found out what he is like. I didn't send this message to him - it was supposed to have been within a private area so it is his fault for snooping. If he had respected my privacy he wouldn't have been offended. So I make no apologies as infringing my privacy is more serious.

They couldn't take the matter any further because I had more of a claim against him for invasion of privacy and that it was a setup to reveal the truth.

He didn't accept me for months afterwards.

v. Same Difference - Channel 4 Documentary

At around 1990 I was asked to be interviewed on the Channel 4 documentary Same Difference regarding how The Sheltered Placement Scheme was being used and how it helped some while undermined others. I was the most undermined one on the program. MGSSD refused to be interviewed.

vi. NALGO - Not A Lot Going On

Throughout all this prejudice and discrimination I was a member of NALGO and they never helped me at all. One excuse was "You are not a normal employee or in normal employment", so why did they take my membership fees for a service they weren't prepared to provide?

Over the years I have noticed that trade unions are not interested in getting me a fair deal - the ones in charge are typical of the pretentious and just there for their own glory than helping get a fair deal for all. How many take advantage of their position for their egos and take as much as they can out of it?

vii. Disablement Resettlement Officer In Pontypridd

Also the Disablement Resettlement Officer based at Sardis House in Pontypridd never did his job properly. He was supposed to help me progress and see how things were going but never did it. When I confronted him I was told that if I refused to stay on The Sheltered Placement Scheme I would be out of a job. It was a way of holding me to ransom by these cowards. Little did they know I was going to get away from their stranglehold in 1993 and eventually the truth of all what they were doing was to come out when I could prove I was held back and not incapable like they were implying.

viii. IQ Test At My Dopiest

Around 1990 although I had already got an IQ of over 150 I decided to sit another one when I was on the maximum dose of anticonvulsants allowed to be prescribed to a patient. This had a significant effect on making me tired and doping my brain but still managed to score 142. So

142 was my IQ at my dopiest. I have tried to get this information from MENSA using the Data Protection Act as they should have records of it somewhere but they don't even acknowledge my query. If they haven't got courtesy to reply to my request they aren't good enough morally.

ix. Moving On Or Suicide

Anyway, I was getting used to being undermined and not recognised so the thought of suicide was increasing. I felt the world was going against me and was looking for every opportunity to blame me for others faults and if you watch The Weakest Link you will see how so often cowards gang up with their votes on the strongest to make the strongest look the weakest because the strongest is too good and too much a threat. I wouldn't want to go on this show as I would fear being treated like this and it would reflect what I went through.

I had taken several minor overdoses (not quite enough to cause permanent damage but to get myself heard) in an attempt to get myself heard. Also after days of undermining in work, blame for others problems and then being pushed about by other commuters, I was ready to explode. Sometimes I would start smashing things up around the house; putting in windows and threatening more disruptive action and retaliation if I continued to be treated like this.

I was beginning to feel that I was going to end up in trouble and if I got a criminal record for defending myself and seen as the wrongdoer I would give up work, make myself too ill and become a burden on the state inflicting even more self-harm on myself.

I was getting fed up with corrupt charlatans in high positions of authority subjecting me to continuous oppression so I wanted to do something to break away from their stranglehold as well as later on expose what they did – which I am doing now.

Therefore the urge to get somewhere and make a move got stronger and we decided that given the way things were happening it was in our interest to go through a lot of upheaval and take a risk for a better time ahead so we decided to relocate and moved up to Lancashire. Things couldn't get much worse, so the chances of some improvement were very likely.

It is obvious I was being subjected to persecution and oppression to suppress my progress as there was no way I was less capable than the average person, so these useless currants in authority were using the epilepsy to undermine me – they probably felt better because they could exercise false one-upmanship over someone with the potential of a genius, although it wasn't genuine – but it never is with the privileged and perverted.

x. Maths Is Still Not Promoted For The Disadvantaged

Maths seems to be a subject only the privileged are recognised and supported in for with so many in ordinary schools being under-taught. Nowadays, many Welsh employers are concerned at the lack of mathematical skills demonstrated by employees. ESTYN's report said maths was the lowest performing core subject at key stage four - when pupils work towards GCSEs - and the lowest in the UK. Chief inspector Ann Keane said some employers had to invest in numeracy skills training for school and college leavers.

Well I managed to prove my potential and connection with genius and natural talent, not through being ponced-up, like so many in high positions. If they cannot value those from poorer or disadvantaged backgrounds who stand out then those sick and twisted individuals in authority who undermine them have only themselves to blame (not the school-leavers) as they are responsible for undermining talent and not letting talent go to better use.

There must be many youngsters who are much better at maths than they are perceived at, but they don't get the support they deserve or need simply because it is a subject only recognition is granted to the privileged. Why do disadvantaged individuals who are highly capable get undermined? Because it shows the privileged that cannot perform equally as well as being inferior – even when they have had preferential treatment and this is a double-blow for them.

If I hadn't had the determination to fight and let Mr Brimfield and the authorities rule my life I might not have even got a CSE in maths. Would that have meant I was no good at maths? Just because these youngsters haven't been given a fair chance in life doesn't mean they are not capable – many are probably more capable than many of the toffee-nosed rot at the top.

11. Relocation Into Business

In 1993 we decided on running a small going concern to get away from this stranglehold of employer exploitation and no chance of getting another job. Pretty soon I started getting disability Living Allowance as I was informed of entitlements to it and that I should have been getting it since I left school.

i. Self Employed

We managed a general store and didn't have access to a vehicle. My mother has never driven (other than one driving lesson which she didn't like) and I couldn't so we still managed without a vehicle.

Over the time we came across many spongers and individuals giving sob stories trying to get things for free and if we refused they would get offensive, so we started to get thick skinned and tell them to get help off the state, not come running to us but some were anti-social about this because we didn't give them something. We got to know the tactics of what liars, spongers and beggars try as well as the intimidation some would try to get us to change our minds. There were quite a few feckless customers living nearby who were the most unreliable and would try everything to get out of paying so we had to name and shame them in the window.

We would go out of our way to help customers and while out and about I would try to get some of the less capable of people the things they were looking for. However, like always, some take you for granted and if I don't do what they want they started giving us verbal abuse. Some would get unpleasant if I didn't go out of my way for them and others were offended if we didn't give them credit. Too many would try to get out of paying because they were spongers so I became wise to their tactics.

ii. Pepsi Max Big One - Blackpool Pleasure Beach

In 1994 the Pepsi Max Big One was ready for use and living within two minutes of the park I decided to have a go on the day it was launched. At this time I still had epilepsy but I wasn't bothered as I was strapped in. I was on it within a few hours of it opening to the public but managed to get ahead of the crowds. I lived within about one minute's walk of the entrance to Blackpool Pleasure Beach. I went on it numerous times and it was an experience. It didn't bother me but many ordinary people couldn't stomach the ride.

iii. Moving On

The next section is brain surgery and since being cured of epilepsy I haven't been involved in such violence as before, but I still get into big arguments and tend to use my voice more. I have become more foul mouthed as this is the way I let my frustrations out without violence. I still argue to such an extent I have driven people to tears and the verge of breakdown or suicide (or so they claim - maybe a tactic to try to win) but I have no consideration for such people who try to make me look in the wrong and I won't let the mater rest until I have got justice or revenge.

I also have no regrets at my behaviour and the disruption and violence used over the years. This was all in defence and survival against unacceptable oppression and controlling tactics of others who were stubborn and wouldn't listen or reason; and if I hadn't put up a fight my life would have been ruined.

Considering all the disturbances I was involved in I never got into trouble because it was clear I was the victim and I would cause more mayhem if I was a victim of a miscarriage of justice so it was obvious that I could hold a lot more against society than they could against me. If I was ever to be criminalised or taken to court for assault, I would have brought the background into it regarding being emotionally disturbed because of how the state treated me and more, so maybe this was a deterrent not to prosecute me and take it further because once they had done this, I would have spilt the beans and nothing would have stopped me once I got a criminal record. Luckily enough it didn't happen but with the disruptive streak I had if there was no hope in making anything of my life I would have become a major nuisance in revenge at how I had been treated and maybe ended up being locked up again. Think of the way I was at the age of twelve - I was beyond control and had no fear of authority as I was prepared to take on anyone and it took several adults to restrain me so seducing me with Valium was the only way they got control over me, so imagine the determination to fight the evils of inferiority I have within me if I needed to.

When I was in these situations I didn't care about the law or what those with authority over me said - I would do anything to defend myself and make the decisions myself. Apart from scraps during my schooldays when I was a child I have never hit a child and all the violent attacks in retaliation have been at adults since they should have known better.

Knowing what it was like, I have the utmost respect for children and would not even raise my voice at them knowing how cruel a voice can be. Since tutoring I have helped many disadvantaged youngsters and they have found me very understanding when I have picked their brains to try to bring out the talent in them (using my experiences but not mentioning any of it to them). I don't talk of my experiences but use my knowledge to try to comfort those who feel undervalued. I try to get them to realise it is others who are not too happy with themselves who try to undermine them, so they should see their own true values, not accept the devaluing by others.

Why should I look up to those who have been recognised when I haven't received anywhere near the recognition I deserve? I would rather recognise the unrecognised as I am sure some could have done more than the ones most recognised.

12. Brain Surgery

Not long after settling down I started going to The Walton Centre in Liverpool for tests to see whether it would be safe to have brain surgery. This was after applying to the local health authority and getting approval for the funding. If the authority thought I wasn't worthy of it they could have stopped me from having the treatment.

I went through various tests of having one side of the brain doped while the other side was tested. This was done both ways and it was concluded that it should be safe for me to have brain surgery.

On 1st April 1996 I underwent brain surgery and was wondering if I was going to end up the biggest April Fool out. I was in hospital for a week and then everything was fine and I was discharged.

This was the date new authorities were formed across the UK and Mid Glamorgan County Council (MGCC) split up into unitary authorities. So throughout the time MGCC existed (1974 to 1996 and a year before) I had epilepsy throughout and was cured the day after it didn't exist any longer. MGCC had gone, and the epilepsy had gone too.

On the evening of the surgery I had a book about places around the UK to keep myself connected with the outside world and decided to put my memory to the test. I had often wondered how to spell Llanfair PG in full (Llanfairpwllgwyngyllgogerychwyrndrobwllllantysiliogogogoch) so I decided to learn it that evening and tested myself the next morning. I have managed to remember it clearly ever since.

i. EastEnders In Blackpool

Later in 1996 while I was recovering, EastEnders was visiting Blackpool and I saw Tiffany and Bianca with a crew filming around the Pleasure Beach. Near to the end of September it was on BBC and I could be seen in the background. I have been seen on TV a few times and had my photograph in a national newspaper, so have had a little bit of fame.

ii. DWP Doesn't Let Patients Properly Recover

It took getting on to a year to settle down to a new way of life and be convinced the surgery was successful. There were many gut feelings of fear but they soon disappeared. By spring 1997 I was ready to make a bigger move and progress.

However, before I had time to fully recover the DWP was trying to take me off my DLA - they seem to expect someone who has had part of their brain removed and having to adjust to a new lifestyle to be available for full time work within two months of brain surgery without being able to recover.

I don't think brain surgery would be applicable to workers within the DWP as it would be something more like sponge surgery they would need. Most of their capabilities are hollow and inflated filled with loads of gaps.

This department doesn't seem to care about acting in the best interest of claimants.

13. New Labour New Discrimination New Hatred

When New Labour got into power, Tony Blair promised "A fair deal for all" and "The chance to make the most of one's potential". This sounded exactly what I needed but unfortunately none of this was true. What happened was yet more discrimination in favour of overpaid cheats and to the detriment of gifted, underpaid and highly talented workers who have been exploited like slaves.

All government policies seem to add insult to injury since I get left out or treated unfairly when compared with others – all because of what government departments did to me during my years of development. So is it a conspiracy by people in high places to suppress the progress of highly capable individuals from poor backgrounds?

i. Underqualified Then Suddenly Overqualified

Although with no proper career experience behind me I wanted to move on and go for some other training but all of a sudden I was overqualified in spite of having no more qualifications when I had epilepsy and was treated as underqualified throughout this time.

Being overqualified meant I wasn't entitled to any financial assistance to kick-start my career and yet there were others who were in their early twenties who were underqualified and earning over two and a half times the salary I was on who could get some financial assistance off the state to boost their career.

ii. Labour Supporting The Spongers & Charlatans

Where is the justice and fair play in that where someone who has been robbed of their childhood, deprived of opportunities to make the most of one's potential, underpaid and living in poverty who has been betrayed and in need of more support who gets no support for being overqualified, yet someone who has been overpaid, underqualified, living in luxury and had everything handed to him on a plate can get more support? This added insult to injury by a load of bureaucratic charlatans in high places and as a result, I see New Labour (or Labour now) as the party to reward the greedy, feckless and incompetent while penalising those with the potential to do well. A lot of reward for failure came up while New Labour was in power.

I tried on no fewer than nine occasions to contact Tony Blair when he was Prime Minister but I never got an acknowledgement or answer. I pointed out that his pledge to be fair and maximise the chances of using potential didn't yield true with me as due to factors exempting me from support it added to the unfairness I had experienced with no help at all, so I have really got where I am without any support whatsoever - less support than many get handed to them on a plate.

Obviously Tony Blair wasn't interested in ones like me – again because we are too good for them and a threat to their charlatanism. They need to exercise oppression against us to suppress our progress.

As a single, childless male I was treated worse than better-off spongers who had never worked. So I now see New Labour as being the party in support of the greedy, feckless, incompetent and selfish since they always seem to gain at the expense of others even when times are bad; they get what they can when times are good but never pay their share when things get tight but moan and get more -just like the banks.

They must be inadequate to need all this bailing out and support - especially when those who have had it much harder are expected to go without even more for them.

As a result of how I continue to be excluded from getting a fair deal and the support I am entitled to, I have no respect for authority. Also with the expenses scandal where many MPs were found out to be fiddling their expenses and tried to make out it was human error when they were caught shows just how much corruption goes on within government and the deep rot which resides at the top.

14. Continuation Of DWP Corruption

I also tried to get the benefits I had been conned out of backdated from Social Security as I had grounds for an Ex-Gratia payment, but Labour bureaucrats and ministers made me a scapegoat and blamed me for not claiming saying the onus is on the claimant to claim and having a disability doesn't automatically entitle anyone to benefits.

i. Loss Of Notes To Hinder My Case

They conveniently lost my notes to delay progress with the investigation which meant it had passed the time allowed and they could close the case without any justification – another attempt to cover up their wrongdoings

I had evidence that I was entitled to it from school days and there was also written evidence in my mother's files but they chose to ignore this and not give me what I had been conned out of. Alistair Darling, Ian McCartney and other ministers judged against me so I now know how corrupt they are and have no trust in Labour for the added prejudice I have experienced.

ii. Domains With DWPCorruption

I have since acquired the domain name dwpcorruption.co.uk which exposed many wrongdoings which took place within the DWP where claimants were conned or bullied.

It has become apparent that other dwpcorruption domains have been purchased by civil servants within the DWP to stop the name becoming freely available for exposure uses.

- dwpcorruption.com is held by DWP, Market Street, Newcroft House, Newcastle Upon Tyne NE1 6ND;
- dwpcorruption.net is held by DWP, Market Street, Newcroft House, Newcastle Upon Tyne NE1 6ND;
- dwpcorruption.org is held by DWP, Quarry House, Quarry Hill, Leeds LS2 7UA;

- dwpcorruption.org.uk is held by DWP, Room 9202, Benton Park View, Benton Park Road, Newcastle Upon Tyne NE98 1YX

- dwpcorruption.co.uk is held by me.

15. Another Illness Takes A Bite

In 1999 I came off all my medication but it was a risky time as I had just started at where I am still working and by coming off my medication I didn't want to start having seizures again.

Not long after I was fully off my medication my body started to have symptoms of a different kind and I don't know if it was because I had started consuming different things or a withdrawal of the medication my body had been so used to.

In 2001 I was getting pains within my digestive system and my local GP didn't think much of it. I was prescribed some anti-diarrhoea medication but later the pain was getting worse but not unbearable. Later that year I was diagnosed with ulcerative colitis and by mid-2002 the pain was getting worse I was urging the doctors to get me treated.

i. Starting To Drive

While I had ulcerative colitis I was learning to drive and on 11th February 2002 I passed my driving test and this was the start of more freedom but I was in pain for a while and couldn't get out and about freely until this problem had been sorted out. The news got around and many sent me a card for passing. Most of the cards arrived on the morning of 14th February 2002 – I wonder if the postman was curious as to why I was getting so many cards?

ii. Getting Into Hospital

They were trying to fit me in and I was having tests but in November it was so unbearable I sent a fax to the Leeds General Infirmary (LGI) stressing the pain I was in saying I let out screams when I got to the toilet but have to suffer in silence when in public - it was so unbearable I wish I was dead. Within a week I was admitted into LGI for surgery.

Over the months I had been losing weight and was about 11.5 stone (down from 15.5 stone).

When they performed the surgery they saw how much the illness shad progressed and had I left it much longer it could have ruptured and I might have died.

During removal of my large intestine I was in a critical way and my body got infected. I had to have several additional emergency operations and was in high dependency for a week. It later came to light that I had contacted the MRSA Superbug and it nearly took my life.

During my time at LGI there were mentions of Jimmy Savile being around somewhere, but that didn't mean anything to me at the time. He was definitely present when I was in hospital with all the chatter we heard from time to time.

I was in hospital for about five weeks and was home in time for Christmas 2002. My weight then was 9.5 stone and I was very thin.

I was off work for four months until March 2003 and when I got back I was given grief and accused of exploiting sick leave. Most of this time I had the MRSA infection and eventually when it was clear I was let back to work.

iii. <u>The Start Of Real Driving</u>

While I was recovering from surgery I wanted to familiarise myself with driving but now without pain. Obviously this takes a while to get used to driving, but by the end of 2003 I was getting long distances in and before long I had visited most parts of the UK. In 2008 I decided to try my Advanced driving Test and passed this on 27th November 2008.

I have since visited all parts of the mainland of the UK. There are some areas I haven't combed as much – these being Cornwall and the western side of Scotland. I have been around these parts but haven't had time to go in and out the coastline by the western side of Scotland but mostly up the main roads which bypass these places.

16. Moving On And Living Life To The Full

Since 2004 a lot has happened and mostly for the better. There have been some things which haven't been right but then that is life. Driving, going abroad, getting into singing and amateur dramatics, speaking confidently in public, a private maths tutor and champion, advanced driver, I am getting a feel of recognition although some still like to be seen by their position than their skills because it gives them the chance to belittle me.

Most people don't seem to have inflated egos and see me for what I am; but those who try the belittling act can still bring a bit of the problematic side I had from many years ago when I feel they are being corrupt and trying to invert the truth to their advantage.

I have come across many domineering middle-classes who have had plenty handed to them on a plate as well as need constant spoon-feeding to maintain their false one-upmanship. They prefer to be seen by how they appear on the outside but try to hide their internal weaknesses (their real self) while undermining others who appear stronger and therefore a threat.

They have got a lot of hidden weaknesses while we have got a load of hidden strengths. So when the battle commences, we can unleash a lot of this strength and target their weaknesses which they are trying to hide. We are 'bigger' than we are seen while they are 'smaller' than they are seen. This can mean we can be bigger than them, and I have shown this, but because they are ponced-up elitists they won't honour the truth. Their images are often decorations and nothing more than the icing on the cake (a form of make-up, like what ponces need).

Anyway, I have moved on, rebuilt my life, risen above many and getting mixed in with the right kinds. I still intend to get the authorities to accept the truth and that is my main objective for doing this book. The next section is for all the failures and unacceptable actions of the selfish and two-faced.

Name & Shame

17. Equal Opportunities

Equal Opportunities is nothing more than a farce – it is often used to let the cheats and charlatans of society get preferential treatment than helping the ones who are genuine victims of discrimination get a fair chance in life.

Quite often if you are discriminated against it can be because you are too strong and when seeking help you are too strong to get support or have your complaint taken on board and so you experience discrimination in a double way.

The only answer is to take the law into your own hands and deal with it another way. This could make you have a criminal record for fighting for your rights. I didn't care if I ended up with a criminal record for exposing the truth and standing up for my rights when times were a lot worse.

Obviously it is different now as I have a lot to lose, but back then I didn't have much to lose and so I didn't care if I got into trouble as losing my job (which was degrading and what I was forced into) could have been a good thing.

18. Robbie's Law

Robbie's Law gets its namesake from Robbie Powell, who died an unnecessary death at the age of ten, back in 1989. Due to this loophole in the law, at every turn his death has been swept under the rug. His family and thousands of others have endured years of grief, injustice and frustration.

In December 1989, Robbie Powell aged 10, of Ystradgynlais in Wales is hospitalised for four days. He loses 25% of his body weight and is critically dehydrated. The hospital suspects Addison's disease, an adrenal condition that's highly treatable, but will result in death without treatment. Doctors there order an adrenocorticotropic hormone (ACTH) test for the condition, but this isn't followed through. The test recommendation isn't communicated to the Powells, but is communicated to his GPs. Instead the Powells are told by the hospital that Robbie suffers from gastroenteritis caused by a throat infection.

Four months later, in April 1990, Robbie again suffers from vomiting, weight loss and acute stomach pains. He is seen seven times by five doctors over 15 days. None of them perform the basics: check symptoms, do a blood test or refer to the hospital. Only one doctor checks the medical records, containing the crucial warning from the hospital. He dies from critical dehydration as a result of Addison's disease. His death could have been avoided, but due to a combination of mismanagement, dishonesty and deliberate cover-up, none of the doctors are prosecuted.

What followed was a long battle with every judicial, police and governing body in the UK. At every point in this long and painful journey for justice, every door is shut in the Powell family's faces. Not only this, several of these governing bodies fail publicly and spectacularly in their duties to investigate the case.

After taking their case to the High Court, Court of Appeal, and the House of Lords; the European Court of Human Rights in May 2000 erroneously advised the Powells that their case is inadmissible. Their statement to the

Powells reads: “As the law stands now, doctors have no duty to give parents of a child, who died as a result of their negligence, a truthful account of the circumstances of the death. Nor even to refrain from deliberately falsifying record.”

Robbie’s Law and the Duty of Candour were born from a seriously dire need for openness and honesty in healthcare. Robbie’s Law means that healthcare staff must tell patients and their next of kin the truth, when a patient safety incident occurs. Robbie's Law is also a pledge for the care of everybody in the UK. So that when a person is faced with a heart-breaking loss of a loved one, the doctors must tell the truth, and refrain from falsifying medical records.

- If your family member dies of medical error or negligence, do you want the doctors to tell you the truth about what happened?

- Do you want to be treated by a medical system that favours honesty and candour over secrets?

It's shocking but it's the law:

- "Doctors have no duty to give parents of a child who died as a result of their negligence, a truthful account of the circumstances of the death. Nor even to refrain from deliberately falsifying records." European Court of Human Rights (ECHR) May 2000.

19. Epilim – The New Thalidomide

Helenor Bye was just twelve years old when she was experimented on and killed in a drugs trial being carried out in Wales in 1977. Helenor was misdiagnosed with epilepsy and given Sodium Valproate (Epilim in the UK, or Depakote in the US), which was on trial in the UK at the time. In July that year, a few days after playing in a public paddling pool, Helenor became ill and was taken to Bridgend Hospital by her parents Derek and Joan Bye with a suspected bladder infection.

Dr Trevor Hyfyn Jones, the paediatrician treating Helenor arranged for her to have an IVP, (an intravenous pyelogram) telling her parents it was 'normal procedure' to find out if there was any underlying problem with Helenor's kidneys. What her parents did not know was this procedure was very dangerous and could lead to serious side effects.

Helenor remained in the hospital for a total of five days. Her parents were told on the fifth day to take their daughter home. When Mr and Mrs Bye asked what was wrong with their daughter, no one was able to give them a satisfactory answer. Instead, they were ordered to carry on giving their daughter the drug Epilim (Sodium Valproate) to control their daughter's epileptic condition.

Mr Bye trained and experienced in working with those suffering from epilepsy questioned the doctor's diagnosis and asked Dr Jones how he had been able to diagnose the condition without performing a full EEG examination. Instead of receiving a polite explanation the family were threatened and told that if they did not agree to the prescription of Epilim, Helenor would be removed from them by Social Services.

Faced with the prospect of losing their daughter, Mr and Mrs Bye requested a second medical opinion but this request was denied under the threat of intimidation. The Bye family left the hospital after Dr Jones reluctantly agreed to monitor Helenor's progress on a monthly basis. Dr Jones only agreed to this however, if the Bye family agreed to maintain a dosage of

800mg per day, telling them that it would be dangerous to withdraw the drug or stop it instantly.

Mr and Mrs Bye said that from this point they watched their beloved daughter Helenor progressively deteriorate as she began to suffer the horrendous side effects of Epilim. Within weeks, Helenor began to suffer from sleeplessness and coordination problems. Despite this and the fact that Helenor had lost a lot of weight due to continuous vomiting, the paediatrician advised her parents that this was nothing to worry about and her body was adjusting to the medication.

The truth was that Helenor was slowly being poisoned to death and her symptoms were an early sign that she was extremely ill, something that should have been obvious to Dr Jones.

Instead of recognising the documented adverse reactions to Epilim however, Dr Jones decided to blame Helenor's severe weight loss on the slimming disease anorexia nervosa and psychiatric problems referring her to a psychiatrist!

On Friday, April 21, 1978, Helenor, emaciated and weighing a mere three-and-a-half stone, was taken back into Bridgend hospital, with Epilim poisoning. (Hospital records record Epilim toxicity.)

Dr Jones, obviously realising his error immediately withdrew the drug, despite knowing that this was dangerous!

In a bid to cover up the truth, the hospital butchered her little body and stole her organs, telling her parents that she was still alive.

Today, over three decades on, her parents are still fighting for justice for their beloved daughter.

20. The Bridgend Suicides

In 2007, a number of youths started taking their lives in the Bridgend area and three of them were within walking distance of where I was living when I was down there. In 2008 Bridgend was globally recognised as The Suicide Capital of the UK and suicides continue to happen in the most deprived areas. My experience together with Derek and Joan Bye's all happened in the Bridgend area.

All the suicides seem to come from neglected estates where there was no hope for the youngsters in these deprived communities; and having attempted suicide when I was their age in the area (for similar reasons under different circumstances) I tried to find out why this had happened.

Was it a failure by the state, betrayal or neglect? It is alleged that some of the victims could have been experimented on and the authorities are trying to keep quiet about it. I tried to contact Carwyn Jones, First Minister for Wales who is from the Bridgend area about my concerns but like Tony Blair he hasn't acknowledged.

I have visited every community I lived in and more recently as a visitor calling into various pubs as a visitor. Most probably didn't know I had already been living down that way and I probably have more knowledge of the area in general than the locals.

One pub a local friend and I went into in Bettws was The Oddfellows Arms and a pub quiz was on. We were welcomed and took part but didn't do too good or too bad. Not long after, it was connected to one of the suicides.

I regularly visit different communities within the Bridgend area as I find the people very friendly generally. It was only a handful of sick and twisted individuals in the authority and public sector responsible for what I went through and I had many days escaping and appreciating my freedom. Many communities give me memories of my freedom where I went around as a stranger but under the fear of possibly having a seizure. If I got out for a day without incident it felt great.

I also have some great memories before the problems started and these are better than the later ones I have of having moved on. Anything before all this started is much better than the memories I have now as I have too many upsetting memories to live with now. So my earlier childhood in the Bridgend area has some comforting thoughts.

Unfortunately today, Bridgend has one of the highest depression, mental health and suicide rates in the UK, with many of them being put on psychiatric drugs and the females having babies with birth defects.

i. Carwyn Jones

I have tried to contact Carwyn Jones over concerns of the suicides of vulnerable children in the Bridgend area after how I had been treated while living in the area. I have suspicions that they might have been abused or experimented on (like I was) and couldn't face up to reality after these experiences.

Carwyn Jones inherits ultimate responsibility for what happened in the past by the authorities in Wales and any reluctance of government bodies refusing to assist with my investigation into why I was treated the way I was.

Going by others who have suffered at the hands of public services in Wales such as the "Justice 4 Linda Lewis Campaign" where there appears to be a cover-up of what happened with all victims.

Why don't these people who are supposed to represent the general public pay attention to these failures, acts of neglect and abuse? Have they got something to hide? It is more likely that they will have something to hide than the ordinary worker within society. Who knows what they get up to at the top when they think they don't have to report or justify anything to anyone because they are on top – especially if they were once lawyers?

It is apparent that the abuse of children is and has been for a long time been high on the agenda of the sick and twisted individuals who masquerade as politicians who should be accountable to us within positions of public service.

The treatment of Linda Lewis' daughter by those in positions of authority more than proves this.

It is obvious to us that Carwyn Jones is one of, if not the main man responsible for keeping "Justice 4 Linda Lewis" from being achieved.

Is it no wonder that he does not reply to any emails sent to him here.

Silence is a clear admission of guilt and a lot to hide.

For The First Minister of Wales who is also the Elected Assembly Member for the town of Bridgend, which has the highest number of teenage suicides in the UK, Carwyn Jones' doorstep is the hell hole of Wales. We will never discover the high levels of suicides in the Bridgend area as this man keeps the lid on it.

Carwyn Jones has never replied to emails regarding the Linda Lewis case and consistently avoids the Bridgend Suicide Question. What does this tell you?

Plus he used to be a family court solicitor in Swansea. Join the dots folks. It's not difficult.

Were the killing fields of Bridgend part of an experimentation programme for the acne killer drug?

C'mon Carwyn own up.

Could this be why Carwyn Jones doesn't want to acknowledge my correspondence?

21. The Kendall House Abuse

There has been a lot of abuse of vulnerable people, especially children in care and I came across Teresa Cooper who had experienced being experimented on with drugs, abused, raped and more; and the authorities wouldn't listen to her, so she has put up a battle to get her medical records as well as expose what has been going on but has met up with a lot of reluctance from those responsible. Many of the girls experimented on have given birth to babies with genetic defects, and these have been linked to the drugs the girls were given.

Teresa's books "Trust No One" (ISBN: 0752893300 ISBN-13: 9780752893303) and "Pin Down" give the complete story. Also her website http://www.no2abuse.com has all the information, plus much more.

i. Church Of England

Kendall House in Gravesend, Kent was run by The Church of England and Teresa has tried to get previous The Archbishop of Canterbury (Rowan Williams) to apologise but he ignored Teresa and so an attempt to get The General Synod to listen was also ignored. I have written to both of these and the new Archbishop Justin Welby about what happened to Teresa and the other girls but they haven't shown any response as if they are trying to brush it under the carpet.

5th March 2013

Dear Mr Welby,

Child Abuse – Exposure Of The Past And Protection For The future

This is my third letter to you – the first one was acknowledged but I haven't had anything since you came to office; the second one I sent last month, so this is my third.

In the wake of all the allegations against Jimmy Savile and other figureheads going as far back as the 1960s, with the aid of the internet many victims are coming forward and I read of plenty on Twitter and Facebook.

Kendall House Abuse

One particular matter concerning many girls back in the 1970s is The Church of England's Kendall House in Gravesend, Kent where girls were sexually and physically abused, and forced to take medication (experimented on) which has resulted in birth defects of their children.

Whilst this has affected quite a number of girls, one in particular is Teresa Cooper who speaks for all concerned and written a book Trust No One. She managed to get somewhere with The Synod, but it didn't properly accept liability or admit what had gone on. I am a friend of Teresa and we have discussed our experiences as well as plans to expose more of what has gone on.

I wrote to The Synod and got a reply along the lines of "It doesn't matter to you – everything has to go through Teresa". This is a way of funnelling all support through one person to cover up how popular Teresa was in taking action.

Let us say there were 500 complaints – if we all complained individually it would have some impact, but The Synod would say we have to go through Teresa which looks like one complaint. This is a way of dampening down support.

Sorry but The Synod is corrupt – and we have heard of yet more sexual abuse committed by priests, vicars, etc. so maybe there are perverts in The

Synod or higher ranks within The Church of England trying to cover up what went on and they are afraid – just like other stars now Jimmy Savile has been exposed.

I used to be a regular church goer as a Catholic, but with all the perverts involved in both Catholic and Church of England I don't go to church now. I see church as a breeding ground for perverts.

As victims of abuse many of us are getting together to get ourselves heard and with the internet we intend exposing as much as we can, so if peaceful ways of getting this abuse looked into isn't going to work we may have to consider other ways like how the BBC has suffered. Naming and shaming we will do if we have to, and reluctance to acknowledge our objectives will be seen as perverting the course of justice since in principle this is what it is when someone in a position of authority tries to abuse their power to suppress someone's attempts to get justice. We will gather every possible shred of evidence and piece it all together.

We need a full investigation into Kendall House – like the Jersey Youth Hostel and North Wales Home, so why not look into what happened at Kendall House?

I look forward in anticipation to your cooperation in this matter – for the sake of past victims and prevention in the future; but if I do not receive a reply then I will have no other option than to believe there are yet more cover-ups within the religious institutions as we are hearing all the more sexual impropriety and abuse of young children coming to surface now.

Reluctance to cooperate with victims and their families/friends in uncovering the truth and refusing a proper investigation normally means a cover-up and all this stubbornness will be exposed on various blogs on the internet together with the full story of what happened and all the reluctance exercised by The Synod, which will let readers decide on what is and has been going on within the religious institutions – and it is not very good at the moment.

If you don't answer my correspondence, then your reluctance will mean you need to be shamed for ignoring the issue as well as lack of courtesy. Human error or lack of courtesy cannot cover up wrongdoings which are going on and we intend exposing every bit of abuse or wrongdoing we come across as well as piecing together elements of reluctance to be open about what has been going on – which hopefully will encourage others to start investigating in these areas too.

Thank you very much.

ii. Don't Get Pickled By Eric Pickles

Teresa has also written to her MP Eric Pickles who has also been reluctant to cooperate or show any consideration towards Teresa, so I wrote to him and he hasn't even acknowledged me.

Towards the end of September 2013 when Teresa managed to confront him he answered her telling her to change her medication. Eric Pickles has been criticised for furthering mental health prejudices after he told a survivor of alleged child abuse to "adjust your medication" when she accused him of ignoring her. The Independent reported:

The Communities and Local Government minister made the comment in a recorded confrontation with constituent Teresa Cooper earlier this month. Ms Cooper was one of at least six women who say they were drugged as teenagers at the Kendall House care home, Kent, in the late 1970s and early 1980s, whose children now have genetic defects.

Confronting Mr Pickles, who is her constituency MP, she said: "Nothing has changed on the Kendall House abuse. Only you have ignored it. You have ignored it." Pickles then interjected, shouting: "just, just, adjust your medication".

The two met while at a wildlife event in Ongar, Essex, on 14 September and Ms Cooper recorded the conversation. Ms Cooper, 46, said: "I was shocked to be honest. He's implying I'm mentally ill which is really rude of him because people do have mental health problems and they should not be spoken to that way."

She added: "The Conservatives say 'we need to change attitudes about mental health' but clearly they need to start with Eric Pickles."

Paul Farmer, chief executive of the mental health charity Mind, said: "It is disappointing that a minister would use language that can feed the prejudice around mental health. We would encourage everyone to really consider the impact of using mental health language in a way that could contribute to fuelling stigma."

Mr Pickles' adviser said that the comment was said in "the heat of the moment" and was his way of giving a blunt piece of advice. Mr Pickles had corresponded with Ms Cooper about some of her concerns but she claims she has been trying to speak to him in person for 16 years.

Mr Pickles said: "It was never my intention to insult Teresa Cooper. I was giving her a frank piece of advice in private."

Marjorie Wallace, chief executive of mental health charity Sane, said: "It's a very thoughtless phrase which could be very hurtful. It may be exaggerated out of context, but whatever the provocation, it's a ghastly phrase which should never be used."

Eric Pickles didn't see Teresa in private, so he is trying to make it look as if he has put effort in to listen to her. Since this, Mr Pickles has been trying to discredit Teresa and freely handing out her details to other bodies, which under The Data Protection Act is illegal.

It has also come to light that Eric Pickles tried to get elected in Wandsworth when Teresa was in care there, but he didn't succeed. So instead he got friendly with some of the senior people in Wandsworth council – the ones responsible for the way Teresa was being treated.

In the late 1970s Wandsworth, more than any other council, was to be the model for Eric Pickles - not just in terms of the results of its policies, but also because the then Wandsworth Tory leader, Christopher Chope, was to become a close personal friend of Pickles.

So could this be why Eric Pickles is in one hell of a pickle about what happened in Wandsworth when he was there? He has certainly been a pain in the pickles.

Here is a letter I have recently sent to him:

1st October 2013

Dear Mr Pickles

<u>Teresa Cooper - Child Abuse Kendall House</u>

I am contacting you today as a result of the degrading and insulting comments you recently made to Ms Cooper, a victim of child abuse, who as her MP you have completely ignored and led her along misleading routes in your attempts to discredit her.

For years you have ignored Ms Cooper, and then you tell her to "Change her medication"; and more recently stated in a local newspaper that you have no intention of apologising for your remarks. I have tried to make contact with you but with no success.

You know she along with some other girls who went to Kendall House were abused, raped and experimented with drugs which many of them have had babies with birth defects worthy of drug abuse imposed by doctors and psychiatrists at Kendall House.

As a Member of Parliament, it is your duty to represent your constituents and act in their best interests, even if it is in conflict with your departmental links. Also, acting the way you have by trying to side-track Ms Cooper and not honouring the truth surrounding Ms Cooper's experiences, you have acted in a manner worthy of gross misconduct. But them MPs get away with most of their wrongdoings as many get whitewashed – like so many were in the expenses scandal.

So as a result of the negative impact you have had on Ms Cooper, you are going to be named and shamed in my publication alongside with Rowan Williams, Justin Welby and The General Synod as Kendall House was a property run by The Church of England and they have been as ignorant and arrogant as you refusing to honour the truth and reply. I shall send you a complimentary copy of my publication with details of your reluctance to be reasonable and showing no respect towards Ms Cooper.

I am a friend of Ms Cooper and also a survivor of abuse – a different kind – and my aim is to expose the evils of inferiority associated with false one-upmanship, abuse of status, wealth, power and control, which gets committed by people in positions of trust in authority who abuse their power mostly on vulnerable people who are easy to manipulate and too afraid or incapable of speaking out. They are mostly weak people in high positions within authority who pick on supposedly weaker people; or to put it another way, small people standing on higher platforms trying to look bigger, and the only way they can come over bigger is to abuse others. Think of cowards on The Weakest Link where they (ab)use the power of the vote to make the strongest look weakest which is an inversion of the truth. This is what people in positions of authority do. They (ab)use the power of their authority to invert the truth and make wrongdoers look in the right and victims look like criminals.

Even if you reply to this email, you will still be included in my publication as what you have done cannot be undone – and my intention of naming and shaming you will not be undone either. I am afraid you have got yourself into one heck of a pickle here.

One last point, all the cases of abuse, etc. Ms Cooper has taken up against Kendall House have been proven to have happened, so they are no longer alleged since they have been proven to have taken place. Ms Cooper shouldn't have the evidence discredited in order to have to prove herself again. She has already proven herself and if you cannot accept this then it is clear you cannot accept the truth and shouldn't be an MP as you lack integrity.

As you don't seem to care about insulting Ms Cooper then I don't care if I insult your integrity with the truth.

Regards

Come on Eric, stop getting into a pickle.

22. The Hollie Greig Campaign

In the summer of 2000, Hollie told her mother, Anne, that she had been repeatedly sexually abused by her father, Denis Charles Mackie and her brother Greg. The abuse had begun when Hollie was just six years` old. Hollie said that Greg had also been abused by his father.

Anne Greig reported this immediately to the local police station in Aberdeen. During the course of that summer, Hollie, who has Down`s Syndrome, began to provide more names of abusers. It is alleged that Denis Mackie had been sharing his daughter with a ring of sexual abusers, which included a serving police officer with the Grampian force, Terry Major and an Aberdeen sheriff, Graeme Buchanan.

Robert Green was jailed in Aberdeen for reporting the story to the public.

The Uncle of Hollie Greig was brutally murdered with what appears to be an axe handle. He was found dead in a burning car in a situation that appears to be arson. This was a few weeks after he reportedly walked in on Holly being sexually assaulted by her father.

It is alleged that Scottish Lord Advocate, Elish Angiolini, has illegally used her influence to shut down any investigation and publicity of the Hollie Greig case. It is also alleged that the Scottish Law firm of Levy & McRae has illegally sought to intimidate and influence witnesses and investigator Robert Green for reporting the matter.

Alex Salmond, First Minister of Scotland has been made aware of Angiolini's methods and has failed to act in a way conducive to justice in these cases.

The members of Scotland's Parliament have also been made aware of these injustices and have failed to take any action.

One of the most active campaigners Robert Green was jailed in 2012. The Hollie Demands Justice campaign very much regrets the decision of the Sheriff Court in Stonehaven to deprive Robert Green of his Liberty.

Despite breaches of Mr Green's human rights and repeated irregularities in law and process by the police, the legal profession and the court system since Robert Green was first arrested in February 2010, the Sheriff Court in Stonehaven, Sheriff Principle Edward Bowen saw fit to curtail his freedom, sentencing him to 1 year in jail (9 months for Breach of the Peace, 3 months for Breach of Bail conditions).

Robert has been a most robust and valued campaigner on behalf of Hollie Greig and her mother Anne, in seeking justice for the wrongs inflicted upon Hollie, exposing the lack of a duty of care from those in positions of trust, the perjury of Grampian Police and highlighting the nefarious nature of the legal system and the Establishment in both Scotland and England.

Far from seeing the jailing of Robert as a setback, the Hollie Demands Justice campaign will be stepping up the pressure as Anne Greig will now vigorously move forward with her High Court appeal and is currently discussing the timing of mounting a series of private prosecutions against those who have abused their positions of trust, many of whom have now perjured themselves in the courts and on the public record.

This campaign will not be silenced, it will move forward relentlessly until every possible avenue is exhausted, no matter how long that takes. No stone will be left unturned until Justice is not just done, but that justice is seen to be done.

23. The Jimmy Savile Abuse

When news about the child abuse which took place with Jimmy Savile, it opened the floodgates to get victims listened to who were abused years ago and not listened to or too frightened to speak out. This is where I started filing complaints about a nurse and teacher who both abused me (already mentioned) and the police have looked into them. The teacher case didn't get too far as the way I was treated was not considered to be child abuse back in the 1960s but a form of discipline even though it wouldn't be tolerated today; whereas the nurse who enjoyed injecting me for pleasure went further.

For many years, vulnerable victims were ignored, told to shut up and weren't believed, so speaking out caused more grief. No wonder why so many resort to violence and suicide.

This has given me more reason to detail what I am aware of and explain what could be happening to others who aren't being listened to and when they do get listened to it is too late.

24. Others

The following have failed to acknowledge, reply or meet the standards they are obliged to deliver.

i. Abertawe Bro Morgannwg University Health Board

I have also tried to get my medical records from Abertawe Bro Morgannwg University Health Board but they are putting obstacles to prevent me from getting my notes – they refuse to answer my letters and this appears to be the way that government departments cover up abuse which has gone on within various institutions. They are purposely dragging their feet so that all the wrong which was done can be kept suppressed and they might have even destroyed some of the evidence. Well this book will expose a lot of the abuse the health trust (under another name back then) was responsible for in 1973.

Well, I am going to publicise this in all the talks and publicity I give on how I was treated as the health authority needs to be named and shamed.

ii. Beryl Sharlot

Beryl Sharlot was someone prominent within what was The British Epilepsy Association and she was very degrading towards me. I met her on several occasions and instead of listening or understanding she compared me with The Third World, told me to "Shut up" and be grateful for what I have got. This is typical of the pretentious trying to undermine other stronger people who don't get a fair deal in life, so she continued the persecution - probably because she wanted to be seen as top notch and ones like me are a threat to these pretentious ones. If I should be grateful for what I had then why aren't ones like her grateful for what they have when they have plenty more and always moaning they don't get enough? She eventually became a Chief Executive Officer for the charity.

iii. Blackpool Spiritualist

In 1993, not long after I relocated to Blackpool I was suggested going to The Spiritualist Church in Albert Road so see if anything could be done to help my epilepsy. That evening I had a seizure but it couldn't be helped, so I came again the following week. That week I had a seizure again during the service and was banned from coming because I disrupted the service and they didn't want me anymore. So I don't trust Spiritualism if the attitudes of some are like this. They can simply fogoff.

iv. Britannia Music Company

Back in the late 1970s I was into music and joined Britannia Music Company for its music club where for every full priced album I purchased I could get another at half price and sometimes for every two I could get another free. It wasn't straightforward but I saved up my credits and in the early 1980s Britannia cancelled my membership even though I had continued to purchase albums over the years. I tried to get my membership reinstated as I hadn't cancelled it but Britannia refused and I couldn't exchange my credits for the reduced price and free albums I was entitled to. It looks like it was a deliberate act to con me because I had saved so much up. Never trust Britannia Music Company.

v. Confederation Of British Industry

The CBI (Confederation of British Industry) is highlighting the problem of youngsters with a lack of ability to read, write and do mental arithmetic as well as other key skills. I contacted them to say that while this can be one problem there is a lot of discrimination against disabled people with higher than average capabilities that are treated as if they are less capable than those with inadequate skills and that a lot of talent is going to waste. Have I had an acknowledgement or a reply? No. so I think it is a red herring to side-track from the real wrongdoings going on under the surface within industry. The rot at the top doesn't like those of us who are individual thinkers as we are a threat to their false status.

vi. Emma Turner

Emma Turner from Ewenny near Bridgend advertised as a solicitor for the needs of children with special needs so I wondered if she could help me get justice for what I went through. I contacted her several times but she hasn't given me an acknowledgement or reply. Could it be that my case is beyond her understanding?

vii. Energy Ombudsman

An issue with Scottish Power's meters where the low rate refers to day consumption and high rate for night consumption when it should be the other way round, the issue has been going on since the beginning of the year (January), so I contacted Scottish Power again in October and put in a complaint in October to the Ombudsman Services Energy and got a reply:

"We have reviewed your correspondence and as your complaint has been on-going for less than eight weeks your complaint is outside of our terms of reference and we cannot become involved yet."

I clearly stated in my complaint that it has been on-going since the beginning of the year which means it has been on-going for over nine months.

It appears that when you make a complaint to an energy company and don't get an answer but eventually make a final complaint before going to the ombudsman, your complaint isn't seen as having started form when you first complained but when you put the final complaint in.

No wonder we have such useless and incompetent rot at the top running the country and monitoring standards when wrongdoers are seen in the right and customers get treated like dirt. If I wasn't as meticulous I could have fallen for their mistake and ended up paying much more than I should. I want to protect those who are likely to fall victim but the industry doesn't seem to care.

viii. Every Child A Chance Trust

Every Child A Chance Trust issued a report stating that lack of mathematical understanding and numeracy skills was costing the economy billions of pounds in lost revenue every year. They focus on those not being able to understand the subject. This is just as bad as someone having a connection with a mathematical genius and being treated as subnormal as the talent is going to waste. So I tried to make them aware it wasn't just lack of understanding but also not giving those with the potential to do well the opportunity to use their capabilities to the full. Did I get anything of an acknowledgement or reply? No. those at the top are from a privileged background, which suggests they are false. So it shows they are not really concerned about the cost to the economy but just trying to make themselves look more important than the majority.

ix. Fukipedia

Wikipedia (or Fukipedia as I know it) took off what I had contributed about different types of child abuse and abuse of the vulnerable which had been going on. This was general showing how the vulnerable are normally too weak to stick up for themselves and therefore useless currants are more likely to use such people as stepping stones for abuse as they are more likely to get away with it. Unfortunately, someone objected to what I put and Fukipedia decided to permanently block me. So whoever is behind this is a useless currant preventing the truth from being exposed, and I do not trust Fukipedia as an encyclopaedia for a reflection of the truth. I use Encyclopaedia Britannica which is more reliable.

In recent weeks there has been some news of the demise of Fukipedia as it becomes a bog-standard encyclopedia. Well if it rejects the truth and favours only certain types of information and doesn't treat innocent individuals with respect then good luck to it. I don't like cheap rubbish.

x. Glamorgan University

A team from Glamorgan University in Treforest was looking into abuse of disabled people, and Ruth Northway, professor of learning disability nursing at the University of Glamorgan, said the impetus for the research came from the people with learning disabilities. Ms Northway said people with learning disabilities experience a wide range of abuse, but because they are not educated about the issue, they learn about it from television and the media. They also find if they do try and tell other people they are not believed and if they are believed that's not always acted on appropriately. It happens in the street, on public transport, we had people talking about it happening in the playground with children, within the family home - it's a wide range of areas. I got in touch and they completely ignored me.

xi. Grundig

Around1995 I purchased a shaver but it was damaged and I took it back, deciding to go for another model £10 more expensive but with a £5 refund when you send in your receipt. My receipt had a refund of the damaged one and a payment of £10 to make up for the new one, but Grundig wouldn't pay me the £5 on offer because they claimed my purchase wasn't a genuine sale. I have never trusted Grundig since.

xii. Harriet Harman

Harriet Harman did so much shouting about equality for females; but whenever there was something about equality for males she didn't seem to care. One thing I noticed was that while there were ladies and gents toilets available, it didn't matter about the ladies toilets as they were the full choice; but I came across too many gents toilets with only urinals and no chance to go further. I pointed this out to Harriet Harman and that it was unfair that gents were only being given half their relieving facilities whereas ladies had the full choice.

Did she reply? No.

xiii. Jack & The Beans Talk

During my time trying to unite with other victims to get support and justice I came across Gillian M Bean who is a victim of misdiagnosis within the NHS and helps to run "Sufferers of Iatrogenic Neglect" or SIN. She is one who has to have her say but doesn't seem to listen to others. But then she has been in a director's position of Intertherm Limited in Nottingham and expects others to listen to her.

After being ignored a long time I became more assertive with her and finally she listened to me and we started to get somewhere. I had the identity "Jack" and it was certainly a day to remember when The Beans got round to talking to me as my headline for the day was "Jack and the Bean's Talk".

xiv. Lancaster University

Lancaster University and affiliated colleges – they claim to give anyone with a history of disability an interview for any post applied for - I have applied to get into teaching and promote maths and never been acknowledged, so there are probably some with the mentality of cowards from The Weakest Link looking for excuses to exclude me. Again is it because they are false?

xv. Liberty

Liberty always seems to shout out about criminals and offenders rights but never gave me any consideration when I was fighting for my rights. Why do they support wrongdoers but let victims who have been put through worse suffer?

xvi. MENSA

When it came to MENSA I had already sat a test and scored 142 when I was at my dopiest on the maximum dose of anticonvulsants back around 1990. I recently contacted them under the Data Protection Act about what they may have about me but they haven't replied. So as far as I am concerned I am too good for MENSA as it is for the obvious, not the imaginative since nobody can have their imagination tested at high IQ levels when nobody else has thought of ideas to test the imagination. Someone with a lower IQ with no imagination will score higher because their potential can be measured fully, but only a fraction of mine can be measured and so MENSA's tests aren't good enough. They recognised the normal, not the imaginative. The best are beyond recognition; not all MENSA members are in this category because they have been recognised. It has to be beyond MENSA's assessment for this to apply. Quite simply the best will always be beyond recognition and not all get posthumous recognition when what they thought becomes reality long after they have passed away. I believe I will get recognised long after my death, but as this is after my death then nobody can treat me in the wrong while I am alive as they don't know if it will happen in fact, if it hasn't happened at any point in time, that isn't proof that it won't happen.

xvii. More Double Standards By Government Departments

In 2013, reforms came in for people on benefits. My mother had to give up a lot during her working life and only get a basic state pension. This way she should get her Council Tax (or rates) paid and be entitled to some housing costs as he doesn't own a property and her income is too low. For years I have provided accommodation in my house for her, and her share of Council Tax was paid by the state up until 2012.

Tory reforms made it such that my mother isn't close enough to me for me to claim Council Tax relief for her so I have to pay it in full; but when it comes to charging for rent she is too close to get any support and I am expected to house her for free.

So one way she isn't close enough but the other way she is too close. So she is dependent on me for supporting her; but the HMRC won't accept she has any dependence on me so I cannot get any tax relief for her dependency on me.

So yet more changing the goalposts and betrayal by little people on higher platforms running the country in an unfair way being greedy and incompetent while punishing the decent.

xviii. The Guild of International Songwriters & Composers (GISC)

Some years ago I was helping Paul with his copyright and to get his work recognised, and he being a member of this organisation let me have his username and password to help him out so I got in touch with the organisation directly representing Paul as I could put things over better. Some arrogant, pig-headed official accused me of trying to get services for free under Paul's membership and told me under no circumstances to use their services under his membership.

So helping a friend with a lack of understanding of copyright and other business factors I wasn't allowed to do. Who the hell are they to tell me what to do? If Paul is a member and wants me to help him then I can look at their website under his membership.

I may have joined at a later date with the services they provide, but due to the abrupt way I was treated and accused of trying to get something for nothing when I was helping Paul I never want anything to do with this organisation and they can fogoff for their false allegations and abrupt manner.

xix. Rhondda-Cynon-Taff Authority

Rhondda Cynon Taff (RCT) was the authority which took control of pensions paid into MGSSD. I tried to get my pension transferred over to my new employer but they refused to cooperate and wouldn't let me move it without trying to hold me to ransom. I was denied my freedom of choice to move it because they wouldn't cooperate.

xx. Seren Books, Bridgend

I approached Seren Books as I wanted to give something back to Bridgend but they never acknowledge me, probably because it sounds like it will name and shame Bridgend so I decided to self-publish.

xxi. The Fox Inn At Kelham, Newark-on-Trent

In September 2013, Pat and I arrived at The Fox Inn in Kelham near Newark, Nottinghamshire and got into a parking space seconds before another couple. I could see they were angry at us for getting the space before them and it appears they were out to seek revenge on us.

When we got into the pub, sat down at a free table and were looking at the menu this couple arrived and told a member of staff that they had booked the table we were sat at and we were told to move to another table. There was no reservation at this table we took and so it was a spiteful act to have a go at us because we got to the parking space before they did.

As a result of disgust we decided to leave and I wrote to The Fox Inn's owners (Mr and Mrs Winter) explaining we shouldn't have been moved out from our table as it hadn't been reserved and that this grumpy old couple were trying to victimise us for being in front of them and they didn't get their own way.

I haven't had a reply from the owners apologising for letting the staff exercise discrimination against us because we were in front of them and aiding a couple of selfish and arrogant pensioners.

This is typical of pensioners behaving like overgrown schoolchildren trying to get preference because of their age over others (a minority seeking preference through corruption).

Details of this incident has been reported on various websites. The owners should have apologised for taking the side of the wrongdoing pensioners who were seeking revenge on us for doing nothing wrong. But they haven't apologised, so what does that say? What are these people from Newark called? Think of an anagram.

xxii. The Great British Rip-Off

All of us have to purchase electricity to keep ourselves going and the big energy companies are nothing better than the banks.

They will try everything to rip us off and try to look so innocent, so let me expose a few things which the need to be named and shamed for,

NPower In 2012 when prices went up NPower didn't just increase the cost per kWh but put me onto another tariff when I had a contract agreed with them for several years on a specific tariff – it didn't have fixed price but it was to remain on that tariff. As a result my electricity prices wouldn't have gone up by the advertised amount but more like 50%. So I finished with NPower and changed to Scottish Power.

Scottish Power hasn't been squeaky clean either. Their day meter readings are identified as being Meter 1 and night meter readings as being Meter 2, but on their website it is the other way round. So it looks like they are trying to charge me day rates for night electricity and night rates for day electricity. Since the bigger consumption is at night with the heating and the higher rate is the day rate, it is beneficial for them to charge me the way they do so that they can get more of the higher rates plus less of the lower rates instead of more of the lower rates plus less of the higher rates. 1 x 1 plus 10 x 10 is greater than 1 x 10 plus 10 x 1.

Lastly, it has become more apparent that energy companies sell their electricity to themselves at a much higher rate after buying it from the National Grid. They then claim that this inflated price they pay for it is the cost price and charge customers more. This might be the disguised cost price with themselves being the middle man but the real cost price is what they bought it off the National Grid for which they won't reveal. So if a unit cost 10p and they sell it to themselves for 50p; they then sell it for 60p to the customer claiming to only make 10p when they are really making 50p per unit.

There is a lot of fiddling and disguising figures to make themselves look innocent when they are greedy.

Mobile phone companies are just as bad claiming extra costs to connect with other networks – they are all in it together at high rates claiming it is outside their control and so passing innocent but deliberate price hikes onto the customer.

xxiii. The Institute Of Mathematics And Its Applications

The Institute of Mathematics and its Applications wouldn't grant me Chartered Mathematician Status for all the work I do using advanced mathematics, the private tuition I do to promote maths and all the capabilities I have displayed – simply because I don't have the snob value like the rot at the top - yet there are others who sit on their backsides with high status but do nothing to promote maths and they can get this additional status. So it shows how status stinks.

I have finished with them and so don't put letters after my name. I see people without letters after their name as more genuine and original than many (not all) who splash their letters after their name.

xxiv. The Joseph Rowntree Trust

Like above they are out to help disadvantaged children but because I have managed to rise above many even though I was put through worse than the many they have supported they don't want to know.

xxv. The Monster Raving Loony Party

I lost interest with the main political parties and liked the way the Monster Raving Loony Party took the mickey out of silly politics. For a bit of fun I joined, they took my money but never communicated with me. I made no reference to my experiences but wanted to meet up with some but I didn't get what I had paid for and the few at the top seem to think of themselves as more important, so I now see them as a bigoted clique of overgrown schoolchildren.

xxvi. The MRSA Support Group

The MRSA Support Group I joined after getting MRSA in 2002/2003 and I queried about renewing membership electronically by requesting the sort code and account number as many organisations give this out. One of the committee members was abrupt to me and accused me of asking too much saying it was not in their interest to give out such information. I told them that many businesses do this but he wouldn't budge. Several years later they started leaving their sort code and account number on their website for members to renew and so I queried why the sudden change and why was I doubted. I was told that I asked for a direct debit to be set up – which wasn't true, I asked for the sort code and account number to set up a standing order and so they were trying to side-track from the truth by making out it was something else and I was wrong. I finished my membership with them and they have lost out for making me a scapegoat.

xxvii. The Samaritans

The Samaritans are generally very helpful, but they do have a bad side when they ignore some of us.

When all the suicides in the Bridgend area came to light, it brought back my experiences and I was getting upset. I remembered how I felt when life wasn't worth living with all the punishment I experience for trying while the evil, greedy and inferior always seem to come out on top, so I tried to contact Bridgend Samaritans about my experiences and how it affected me and I wanted to find out more as I knew all the areas where suicides had taken place – some within five minutes' walk of where I used to live. They didn't acknowledge.

xxviii. The Sutton Trust

They are out to help prosperous children from poor backgrounds and would never listen to me I am an example of what happens when we are failed and if they are concerned they should be interested in the outcome and consequences if someone was failed by the state and got no support from anywhere. They seem two-faced.

xxix. Time To Talk

Time To Talk focuses on mental health problems and the stigma associated with it being nothing to be ashamed of. I have a form of PTSD which originated from abuse and trauma in childhood and they weren't interested as they saw it abuse-related and not mental health. All problems associated with mental health occur from some experience so why I was not listened to?

xxx. Tony Blair

As already mentioned, either side of the millennium I tried to make Tony Blair aware that his policies of "A fair deal for all" and "The chance to make the most of one's potential" weren't working for me because factors were being used to deny me a fair deal. Just like back in the 1970s and 1980s my intelligence was used to deny me entitlement for support and my illness was used to undermine my intelligence, my lack of experience and poverty were used to undermine my potential; and my qualifications were used to deny me financial support in spite of living in poverty. Out of all the letters I sent him he never acknowledged one.

Further updates to these incidents and anything new worthy of being published under Name & Shame, the details will appear in later versions. These will be available at http://apaininthers.co.uk.

25. The Coventry Woes

Just like Bridgend, Coventry has had its share of woes in recent years.

I visit Coventry from time to time and go to various pubs, restaurants, etc. to see how things have changed as well as retracing the areas I lived in. some areas I would have to be careful no though as one of the areas I lived in (Hillfields) is a red light area and full of drug addicts so I have been told.

It too has some good memories as many memories are before my problems started; and these are better than more recent ones which contain memories of the abuse I suffer later on in life. So any later memories will have some upsetting parts within them.

i. Family

Unfortunately, I have a half cousin from Coventry who I don't get on with as he has become too bossy and manipulative and he would factuate his beliefs while ridiculing the truth so that what he wanted and said had to be seen as right, denying me my freedom of choice if it wasn't approved by him. Because he factuated his beliefs and undermined the facts on the other side he always wanted the final say and tried to force his preferences on others. I am wrong if I don't do what he wants and he chickens out as he cannot meet me face-to-face when we have a dispute. If he cannot be in control he won't give me the chance to show I am stronger than him – this is why controlling people are chickens when they are likely to lose as they don't want the other side to be seen as the winner so they mess everything up out of spite.

He wasn't alive when I was sectioned back in 1973 and I tried to explain to him that people being too pushy and domineering like he was wasn't very nice for me and I tried to explain. But through his typical stubbornness he wouldn't listen and accused me of emotional blackmail.

This triggered a big dispute within the family and I tried to get him to listen and understand but he was too stubborn to accept the truth and he had to be seen as right. I tried to let him know that being treated that way would make me overreact but he still wouldn't listen and so I did overreact – but I tried to warn him. I will not let ignorance or inferiority take over the running of my life or distort the truth in the favour of the wrongdoer.

Just because he wasn't prepared to accept the truth doesn't mean he had the right to force me to take his side. He was trying to force his beliefs on me while ridiculing the truth. This is where the war between us broke out. He used his stubbornness as strength when it is really a coward's attempt to hinder the stronger side.

He could not win by fair play or treating others the way he expects to be treated. He always expects to be treated better and if he doesn't get looked up at he starts his antics. I posted information on the internet about him and his attitudes, and eventually got threatened by his mother Joan (poor little boy – couldn't stick up for himself) that legal action would be taken against me if I didn't take the information down.

ii. Other News

Also, in 2012, a bar refusing to serve armed forces personnel who were pallbearers at a colleague's funeral due to the fear of them causing trouble. A former pub landlady from somewhere else who wants to remain anonymous said most service personnel were troublesome. "After a few incidents involving army personnel I did try and refuse them entry as nine out of 10 times trouble would break out. Surely questions should be asked about why these serving members of the forces feel the need to go out and get blind drunk, fight and then end up crying!"

Coventry City Football Club has had trouble over paying its rent and is in financial difficulties. Some of the family were Coventry City supporters.

The murder of the four-year-old Daniel Pelka who was beaten and starved to death by his mother and partner happened in Coventry.

Power In The Hands Of The Weak

26. Learning by Experience

For many years (since 1972 when I was last properly recognised for my capabilities) I have felt very much undermined with a difference. I don't believe that I have genuinely been seen as less capable since if I was I would have been helped a little and not been subjected to all the oppression. So going by how I was being treated, those responsible wanted to make me feel inadequate and by restricting my progress and thought that this would work – but it has driven me to having a more determination to challenge anything that isn't morally good enough I refuse to accept or cooperate with.

People who didn't know anything of me who I have met by chance thought of me as a teacher, a lecturer, a consultant, a policeman and possibly been to public school and Oxbridge. So there are qualities visible on my outside and the negativity is nothing to do with ignorance or human error but down to the mentality of those who are like cowards on The Weakest Link and look for every excuse to undermine the best. It is because of all the deliberate oppression I was subjected to which angered me to such an extent and I wanted to use my potential to the full but wasn't let.

So like prior to the problems starting I was proud of my capabilities and wanted to do well, but for thirty one years (1973 to 2004) I have felt no overall satisfaction in my achievements due to the paltry levels of respect, reward and recognition I received over these years. However, in the past nine years things have settled down and I have managed to get more out of life in more ways than expected.

The truth has always been on my side, so when someone doesn't honour the truth but tries to invert the truth against me for their advantage I can go to war with such people.

When I was treated properly and got the recognition I deserved (which didn't happen long) it brought the best out in me and I was top of the class; but when I was treated inappropriately and made scapegoat for others' problems and undermined, it brought the worst out in me and I sank to the bottom of the class as well as becoming one of the most disruptive and problematic of people with violence and disorder which was not a criminal activity but a form of defence for survival after what I was being put through, so I have no regrets of what I did in order to survive what I went through. It was needed to protect myself.

Every experience I have I learn something else about tactics to make small look bigger than big and win by deception. This makes me come up with more ideas of beating the cheats where possible. You can never progress peacefully with inferiority as it expects to come out on top so you have to use destruction for defence as those who haven't got the capability to progress peacefully and fairly won't listen or honour the truth.

The next section may appear to be having a do at those more fortunate than I have been; but it is not a stab at those who have the potential to do well. It is mostly aimed at those who are cheats, liars, backstabbers, bootlickers, charlatans and creeps who always need preferential treatment and when they succeed they try to make out it is genuine. It is a collection of how cheats, liars, wrongdoers and the useless currants in life try to progress but from different perspectives.

They are ones whose capabilities are not as good as the image they want to be perceived as having by exercising false one-upmanship. It is mostly those who rely on having everything handed to them on a plate; needing constant spoon-feeding and in some cases due to their status and wealth exercise false one-upmanship and belittle people from underprivileged backgrounds – especially those of us who have more connection with genius than they have.

Snobbery is a quantity; giftedness is a quality. It is not in the interest of the pretentious to honour the truth, so that is why they have to progress by not honouring the truth or fair play; and resorting to abuse if they can keep the truth suppressed indefinitely.

Success is not measured by the levels of reward, recognition and respect you get but what you have achieved and overcome – much of which gets ignored. Little people in higher positions standing on higher platforms trying to look bigger are still smaller in reality.

There are three types of achievers:

- The genuine – which most decent people are and I wish there was more of these;

- Cheats are those who rely on the use of inferiority to cheat their way and undermine others;

And

- Inferiorists are those who rely on the use of inferiority to cheat their way and undermine others as well as devalue everything above them. Inferiorists are the worst kinds within society.

Cheats just cheat and have something of a chip on their shoulder to cheat and bring better individuals down but inferiorists treat every unit above them as below them so the more you are above them they more they treat you as below them. If an inferiorist was at level 65 and you were 70 then the 5 above would be 5 below and you would be treated at 60; but if you were 85, then the 20 above would be treated at 20 below and you would be treated at 45.

When it came to how I was treated by people in authority, I was about 95 (in the top 5%) and treated at 25 (in the bottom quarter), so this tells me that they were about 60 and the 35 I was above them was used to treat me at 35 below them. So being at about 60 doesn't say much for them being in executive and senior positions. They must have been cheats with such low capabilities and used inferiority to progress.

27. Inflictions Of Inferiority

I make a lot of references to inferiority. Let me explain what I mean.

Inferiority is where weakness is used to undermine stronger people. Everyone has strengths and weaknesses but some who are weak don't like others who are more capable and have a desire to bring stronger individuals down. They use tactics associated with their weaknesses to inflict negativity on their victim to bring the victim down to below their level. Their strength is inferior to their victim's strength so it is inferiority. If they don't use their weakness to undermine others it is just a weakness.

Take for example how cowards on The Weakest Link use the power of the vote to overturn the truth and make the strongest look the weakest. They are inflicting negativity associated with their inferiority to bring stronger individuals down to below their level so they can succeed. I refer to these tactics as "inflictions of inferiority" and all evil stems from inferiority.

You will see how many people in high places have control of others' lives by inflicting their inferiorities into the lives of their victims.

All acts of abuse are evils of inferiority.

28. Government Departments Try To Be Squeaky Clean

It should be obvious to everyone and definitely my experiences have added to this evidence that government departments are out to get away with any wrongdoing they can and come out squeaky clean where possible – mostly making it impossible for their victims to get justice and a fair deal. These government departments inflict their inferiorities on innocent vulnerable people to suppress the truth and normally get away with it because the victims are not strong enough to fight back or gather the evidence against the departments.

iii. The DWP

The DWP was responsible for conning me out of all these years of benefits (which is obvious they played a part with information on my mother's records) even though I cannot prove they misled me, they are seen as squeaky clean even though it is obvious they knowingly denied me my entitlements and let me be subjected to prolonged poverty.

They are also responsible for the defamation of character I experienced while being on The sheltered Placement Scheme which was a scheme for individuals who were not capable of carrying out basic tasks – or in other words subnormal. This has resulted in a loss of earnings, additional psychological problems and hardship, etc. and it wasn't a mistake but a deliberate attempt to undermine my intelligence because I had epilepsy.

Until I get something in return for all this suffering I will never forgive them.

iv. Abertawe Bro Morgannwg University Health Board

Already mentioned, Abertawe Bro Morgannwg University Health Board which is the health authority responsible for my admission into adults' psychiatric hospital when I was twelve and the abuse I suffered. They are refusing to cooperate and help me get to the truth behind this and so are out to keep the evidence suppressed and make the victims look in the wrong.

v. Others

There are no doubts many other government departments who commit wrongdoing and will not admit to it or even when it is obvious they did there will be no way their victims can get justice.

So those at the top running the country are worthy of being seen as nothing more than rot the way they get away with all sorts of wrongdoing.

Well one thing the rot at the top cannot control is the truth and that is something which really hurts. The truth is the biggest asset behind all victims since it justifies why they get treated so badly as well as how sick and twisted the individuals responsible for these actions are.

29. Inversion Of The Truth

Although I have been treated most unfairly and undermined by cheats, liars, backstabbers and abused by the eccentric and obsessed, I have experienced a range of extremes in life and managed to survive. If my experiences were to be recognised by The University of Life, some of the wisdom I have would be beyond the mollycoddling, spoon-feeding, cradling and protected lifestyles of the privileged that wouldn't be able to cope or survive the slightest without extra protection or preferential treatment. Therefore I would have more realistic and genuine experiences of what life is like and how to cope than many at Eton/Oxford/Cambridge. Qualifications endorsed by The University of Life would be more genuine showing how to survive and cope with life's realities than the many onanists from mollycoddled elitist institutions.

This section is not aimed at less capable individuals in general but those who try to exercise false one-upmanship as well as pick on others because they cannot progress in a proper way and so need preferential treatment, need to cheat, lie and deceive in order to progress. They also try to make their victims look at fault so they can cover up their wrongdoings.

Everyone is equal when it comes to fair play, respect, etc. and we should all be let have our say and wait in turn where necessary. Nobody should be forced to suffer for the selfish gains of others but sadly a lot of this goes on. But some people always want preferential treatment and if you don't agree with their view they try to deny you your view ridiculing it and talking down to you as if they have the authority to decide what is right and punish you if you don't do what they say.

I make a lot of references to inferiority as this is an alternative term to being pretentious – it is a comparison of what the individual's genuine capabilities are with respect to the image they try to be perceived as having, not a comparison with someone else. Thus if someone is pretentious, they are trying to make out they are better than they really are; which means their real capability is inferior to their image. People who are inferior in this context often lack integrity, try to cheat, etc. and are not as reliable as people who are genuine. Some of them have double inferiority and these are the ones who abused or picked on me the most. Like cowards on The Weakest Link who use the power of the vote to override the truth to make the strongest look the weakest, this is the use of inferiority. Inferiority destroys others' lives and is the root of all problems within society.

If you watch The Weakest Link and you see how a group of weak cowards with no real chance of coming out on top use the power of the vote to override the facts to make the strongest look the weakest, and so this is typical of destructive inferiority. Inferiority is the root of all destruction and so if there is no inferiority there will be no problems.

People who cannot compete fairly often have inferiority problems and try to bring others down to progress. All opportunist wrongdoers are inferior because they cannot progress properly and have to wrongdo to progress.

Also, people from poor and disadvantaged backgrounds are often undermined and much better than they come across as whereas the arrogant fat cat or yuppie types have inflated egos and think they are better than they really are. This is why I get on better with the disadvantaged, people or those who work hard for a living rather than those who expect preferential treatment all the time. The ones I get on with deserve better because they are better than how they get treated; whereas the ones I don't get on with are false and act like cowards on The Weakest Link trying to make me look weaker because I am a threat to their false one-upmanship and they have the resources to invert the truth just like cowards have the power of the vote to make the strongest look weakest.

I have also noticed that those who are disadvantaged that I have helped out with maths have far greater understanding than they are recognised for – their confidence has been dented and they feel they cannot do it – but I have managed to get some to do much better and so this proves they weren't given the support they deserved and consequently they have been left to rot as If they are useless while those responsible for these failures in positions of authority continue to get wrapped in cotton wool and constantly spoon-fed to maintain false one-upmanship.

People who are glossier than normal on the outside often have a lot of weaknesses on the inner-self which they are trying to disguise.

vi. Treated As Guilty Until Proven Innocent

I make many references to being treated as guilty until proven innocent since many stubborn control freaks in authority know they are seen as innocent until proven guilty, but in order for their innocence to continue to cover up their wrongdoings they must ensure they never get found out or convicted. This means that they have to undermine every possible chance of being found out – and their victims (or close friends/relatives) are the ones who are their greatest threat, especially if they have the courage and potential to speak out. So in order that they a=don't become a threat, these victims are treated as guilty until proven innocent which means it is quite likely that they will never be believed as it is very difficult to prove you are innocent when you are treated as guilty since all evidence which supports you is ignored and therefore you aren't believed. Only if you manage to break away from the stranglehold they have over the truth with you (like I did) will you stand any chance of being seen as innocent, and by that time those who are guilty will have cleared off or even passed away, like some who caused many problems for me by suppressing the truth have done.

Anyone who has got nothing to hide will see you as innocent until proven guilty; so if you are treated as guilty until proven innocent, it is quite likely that those involved have something to hide and you should become suspicious as to why they are trying to undermine your integrity.

vii. Four Better or Four Worse

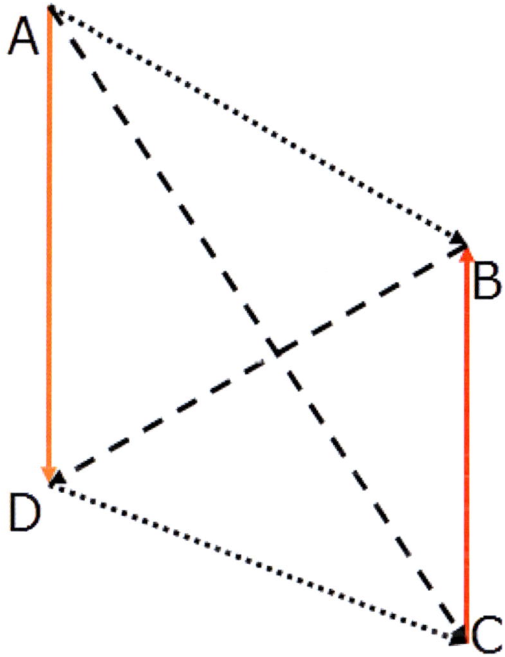

The diagram demonstrates how cheats who apply double standards try to make small look bigger than big and there is no validity or truth in any of their reasoning. Supposing the decent person at A is undermined to D while the cheat at C gets hyped-up to B. we are going to identify all four points whether they are Best, Worst, True or False and show how the comparisons work.

	Individual	Point	Best/Worst	True/False
1	Decent	A	Best	True
2	Cheat	B	Best	False
3	Cheat	C	Worst	True
4	Decent	D	Worst	False

We know that the true values are A and C whereas B and D are false due to corruption, privileges, persecution, external influences, etc. We also know that A and B are the strengths (Best) and C and D are the weaknesses (Worst).

We are now going to compare both levels of the decent individual with both levels of the cheat.

	Decent	Cheat	Best/Worst	True/False	Like or True	Winner
1	A	B	**Best v Best**	True v False	**Like**/False	Decent
2	D	C	**Worst v Worst**	False v True	**Like**/False	Decent
3	A	C	Best v Worst	**True v True**	Unlike/**True**	Decent
4	D	B	Worst v Best	False v False	Unlike/False	Cheat

The first compares Best with Best and for the second comparing Worst with Worst even though not both values used in the comparison are true. This is because of the corrupt world we live in - if it was a fairer less corrupt world we would quite likely have true values when comparing like with like. Therefore, as you can now see, there is only some partial validity in some of the comparisons and nothing in one of them.

The three where there is some validity (like with like or true with true) is where the better individual comes out on top since the stronger side of the better individual is far better than the stronger side of the cheat; and the weaker side of the better individual is stronger than the weaker side of the cheat too. Sometimes the weaker side of the better individual can be stronger than the stronger side of the cheat but normally the stronger side of the cheat is stronger than the weaker side of the better individual. This is why cheats like to be seen at their best and they see better people by their worst in order to exercise false one-upmanship.

When it comes to true values the true side of the decent individual is far better than the true side of the cheat; but the false side of the cheat is only better than the false side of the decent individual. So there is no like for like or truth in the comparison which gives the cheat the top position; whereas the other three which have some truth and would quite likely be 100% (perfect) if society wasn't corrupt give the decent individual the top position.

- A is greater than B
- D is greater than C
- A is greater than C

All comparisons above are valid as the better person is seen as better.

- B is greater than D - the only invalid comparison where the less capable person is seen as better.

Unfortunately, it is only the fourth comparison which gets recognised by control freaks and the truth ignored. There is no valid comparison as we are not comparing like-with-like or genuine values. This is why we have so much rot at the top that control comparisons for their corrupt selfish gain. It shows they lack integrity too.

Coming out on top is a must for control freaks who are obsessed against the truth and exercise false one-upmanship as it is the only way such cheats can feel they can justify being better; but those of us who are worthy of being near to or at the top know so many at the top are cheats, so it is what we are that matters, not where we are on the success scale. If we aren't given equal opportunities we won't bother trying as much as we aren't going to let others take the credits for our efforts while being expected to be used as scapegoats for their problems.

Individuals from affluent backgrounds are more likely to look better than they are whereas the disadvantaged are likely to be undermined; the biggest conflict is between privileged thickos that have a desire to bring gifted individuals from disadvantaged backgrounds down. It seems like you only get recognised for your capabilities if you are privileged but persecuted if you are disadvantaged.

When you think of it, Sir Isaac Newton, Albert Einstein and other major figures were all from somewhat privileged backgrounds and had extra support which helped them get recognised. Going by my experiences I wonder how many disadvantaged individuals worthy of this capability have been undervalued and not recognised; or perhaps as in my case where there was some element of recognition got persecuted so that their progress would be impaired because they weren't from a privileged background? I have reasons to believe that those who do get recognised without a battle are cheats. If I eventually get recognised it won't be through privileges but survival of the fittest.

viii. The Red Hat Which The Privileged Wear

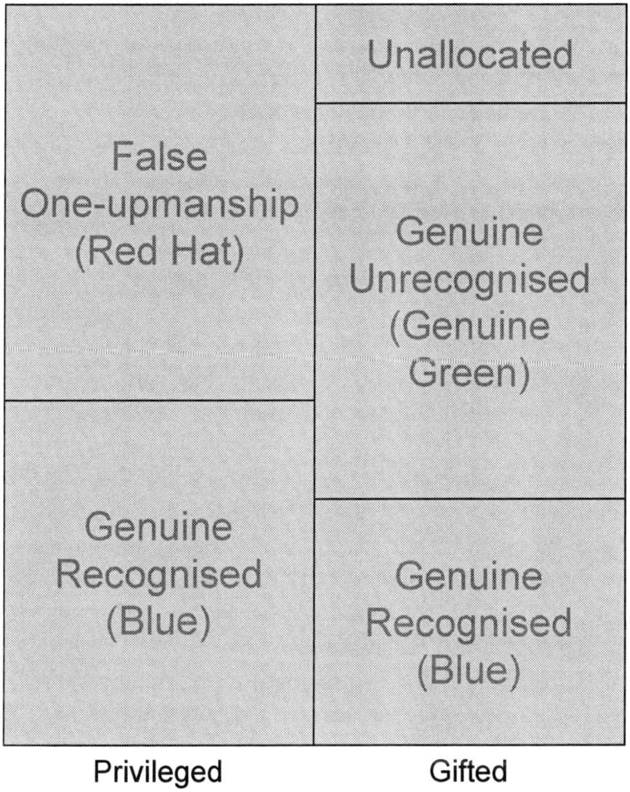

Here we have the privileged whose capability is the blue but wears an element of false one-upmanship on its head (Red Hat) with a bit of unallocated space above; but on the other side we have someone who has capability worthy of both blue and green but is only recognised in the blue because the green area is where he is too good for the privileged. The green area is known as Genuine Green area. This example is for illustrative purposes only and you don't have to be privileged to wear a Red Hat – all you need to do is to cheat on others and try to make out you are better than you are. Many people from all walks of life do this but it is more prevalent in the privilege that only get where they are through having a head-start or being cradled everywhere.

The Red Hat is the false area of the privileged (or the false hat they wear) as there is no genuine capability here – progress is all made through preferential treatment, spoon-feeding, all handed on a plate; whereas the Genuine Green area is the suppressed area where the potential of the gifted and disadvantaged is undermined and ignored. The Red Hat is also the area where all abuse, wrongdoing cheating and corruption takes place.

Quite often, those in positions of authority with power and status use their Red Hat to undermine the others not recognising their Genuine Green area; however many victims will realise they are being targeted and feel so angered by deliberately not being recognised they will use their Genuine Green area as an area for belligerence, revenge, challenges and generally problematic behaviour.

The Genuine Green area of the gifted will target the Red Hat of the privileged and this can result in problems lasting for years where the privileged are too stubborn to accept the truth and the gifted is determined not to give in. sometimes the gifted will be driven to despair through the persecution but some who manage to survive become wise to what goes on and can tell the tales of their experiences to make others more aware of what the privileged perverted do to many disadvantaged and vulnerable people within society.

The more pretentious a privileged individual is, the bigger their Red Hat; and similarly the more a gifted individual is undermined, the bigger their Genuine Green area. When a highly pretentious individual tries to abuse a severely degraded gifted individual there is a lot more mayhem and unrest since both sides are mostly ready for war with each other. I know this from my experiences when I was in my teens and younger adult life.

ix. Difference Between Inferiority & Handicap

Everyone has strengths and weaknesses, and some people have something which may not function properly thus being a handicap or disability. These are all internal and within the individual concerned.

However, an inferiority is not a handicap, disability or weakness but an external invasion of negativity from someone else's weakness forced to work in series with the victim's strengths, and consequently their potential (chain) is weakened by this link which has been forced into their chain of life.

Inferiorities are invasions into others' lives and all originate from inferiority of the inner-self within someone who tries to exercise false one-upmanship or needs to abuse or cheat to progress and win. These people are not as good as they want to be seen as so in order to protect their false one-upmanship from being challenged they inflict negativity associated with the real inferiority of their inner-self into the lives of others.

Acts of inferiority include abuse, betrayal, cheating, contempt, corruption, deceit, fraud, impatience, queue barging, and wrongdoing, etc. and gaining at the expense of others or by deliberately making mistakes in their favour. What about the MPs expenses scandal? This shows that some at the top are opportunist wrongdoers who will do anything they think they can get away with and they always have contingency plans to make themselves look innocent in case they are caught.

Many acts of inferiority are where false qualities are used to exercise false one-upmanship. Capabilities and potential are qualities; status, wealth, power, support, etc. are all quantities which scale up the effects of the individual concerned and therefore make someone appear better through cheating or unfair advantage and such individuals get very cocky and abuse their power to try to suppress the qualities of others who are better. Quantities will never be able to take the place of qualities – much like money will never be able to buy intelligence for someone's brain, so money is used to cheat and give some an unfair advantage. Money is a quantity not a quality. Money will never make someone of ordinary intelligence into a gifted person no matter how much support or educating that person gets. Some drivers on the road with powerful cars get ahead, but they don't keep to the Highway Code – they undertake, barge in and abuse the power of their vehicles to come out first thinking it makes them better. They have succeeded through the abuse of quantity (speed is a quantity) to exercise false one-upmanship.

To sum up, inferiority has the following characteristics:

- Inferiority is destructive to society
- Inferiority only benefits the cheats, abusers and wrongdoers
- Inferiority inverts the truth to make small look bigger than big
- Inferiority is present in all acts of wrongdoing and evil
- Inferiority is the root of all evil and privileged/favoured people are likely to substitute quantity for false quality in cheating and getting preferential treatment, so money is connected with fuelling the power of inferiority

x. Inside & Outside

Everyone is what they are on the inside and gets influenced by how they are supported or treated. Internally is like what we all are naturally; externally is how we are nurtured.

We all have strengths and weaknesses, with some strengths being of outstanding levels and even the more capable of individuals have some handicaps which the less capable are one up on. Some poorer individuals can manage to cope in more severe circumstances yet they are seen as less capable because they haven't had the chance to develop their potential.

I am going to look at quality or mass which is what we are internally; and quantity or gravity which is what influences us externally.

You will see how quantity is often used as a substitute for quality and how gravity and mass are both used by some to throw their weight about.

Some of us are good on the inside and get good support; some are good on the inside and get bad support; some are bad on the inside and get good support; some are bad on the inside and get bad support. We will see how support helps but how victimisation hinders.

Think of a tank of diesel or petrol, it has the potential to transport someone hundreds of miles, provide heating, or even a huge explosion. If treated properly it will carry out its proper task (motoring/heating) but if it was to be abused and a spark ignited it in the wrong way, it could explode causing huge damage nearby. Although the tank had the potential to do a lot of good or bad, it was not to blame for the explosion as it was the spark which ignited it. Well similarly for me, the trail of destruction I have experienced with violence and destruction is the resulted of being ignited by abusers - mostly in authority and I became quite dangerous at times.

I was controlled and restrained by physical power, gang power, sedation power and authority power – these are all abusive powers since they are all based on gravity factors (external influences or quantities) rather than natural powers such as giftedness and talents.

Now this is where we shall separate the false from the genuine.

xi. Inferiority – The Root Of All Evil

Individuals obsessed with coming out on top don't like being outdone because they have an inferiority to hide - which is why I was abused so much by the pretentious. So they adopt a win at all costs since they don't have any integrity or standards. They have to be seen as better because of the inferiority of their inner-self which they cannot accept and will go to whatever length they can to hide it. That is why perverts, inferiority and wrongdoing are so closely connected.

Anyone who abuses the power they have at their hands to come out on top or to win at all costs by immoral means or wrongdoing is a pervert. And power in the hands of the weak and obsessed breeds evil because those who are inadequate cannot achieve anything properly without wrongdoing, abusing or deception; and all perverts are opportunist wrongdoers which they need to be in order to exercise false one-upmanship on their victims.

Those who are less capable need money to progress and are obsessed by it as it is their tool to survival. That is why money is seen as the root of all evil when inferiority is the root of all evil; money is what fuels it.

xii. Aggression Is A Sign Of Inferiority

Aggression is for defence whereas assertiveness is for progress.

Those who are weak and obsessed use aggression for success because they have to defend their false one-upmanship Anyone who gets aggressive with me is not defending themselves in the form of survival of life but defending what they fear losing under fair play their false one-upmanship they try to exercise. This automatically means they are cheats.

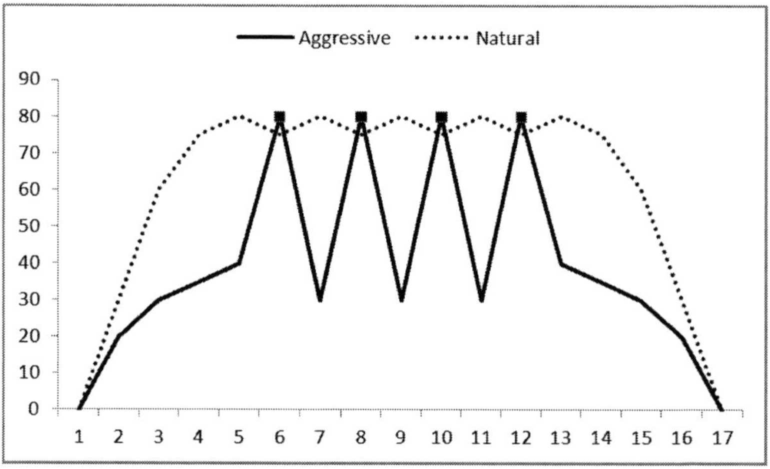

Cheats also have spikes of effort when they use their aggression. These are temporary spikes and don't last long; whereas gifted individuals perform steady and almost constant at a high level. the area under the curve of a consistent gifted person's performance is much greater than someone who is a cheat (much lower generally) with a one-off spike above them through aggression for a few seconds since the area under the spike isn't enough to make up for all the relative inferiority the rest of the time.

The gifted could spike much higher but doesn't feel the need to be aggressive when doing things – the gifted only become aggressive when they feel threatened and need to defend themselves, so aggression is used only as a survival tool and not a competition tool for the gifted. If I cannot progress properly and fairly where I get to where I can peacefully I won't bother trying. I use aggression for defence not progress.

xiii. The Logic Of Inferiority Versus Fair Play & The Truth

This isn't unfair like two people ganging up on one where fair play and the truth are taking on the logic of inferiority, but inferiority is like an infection and it poisons the qualities of others even though its qualities are already poisoned.

Supposing there were ten people all having their fair share of ten per cent and did what they should then this would be okay. But you will see how the logic of inferiority tries to gain at the expenses of others or there is conflict. Supposing the least capable one wanted more, let's say fifteen per cent, and then there wouldn't be enough for it to be applied to all ten so the extra five per cent would have to be taken somewhere from the nine others.

There are three ways to look at this:

- The less capable one insists he is entitled to more and others should go without; if so and all others are to be treated fairly then each of them could apply this argument and look for others to pay the price – including the less capable one – who would be most outraged as his mentality would be for others to suffer for his gain but he wouldn't be prepared to get a taste of his own medicine and lose out for others gains. This would result in social unrest with everyone believing they can gain at the expense of others but others couldn't expect to gain at their expense.

- The less capable one forces the vulnerable or passive individuals to go without and they take it peacefully as they cannot stick up for themselves – this is what goes on a lot within society as many who don't get a fair share cannot stick up for themselves and go without so the less capable can have what is rightfully theirs which they aren't getting.

- The less capable one tries to make someone a victim but the victim stands his ground. The victim doesn't try to have more than his fair share of ten per cent but doesn't let the less capable one have more than ten per cent by taking from him and making him have less than ten per cent. The victim will stand firm and there is conflict with the less capable one trying to gain but the victim not taking it peacefully. The less capable one will try to make the victim look like the wrongdoer when the victim is applying fair play and the truth to the less capable one but the less capable one will object to the defence by the victim. Note the victim is partially giving the less capable one a taste of his own medicine but not doing wrong or victimising the less capable one, just preventing the less capable one from gaining at his expense. This is a bit like a thief taking what is rightfully yours and claiming ownership of it, so you take it back off the thief as it is really yours (which is stealing as far as the thief is concerned) but you have done to the thief what the thief did to you without being in the wrong although the thief will try to make you look in the wrong and look like the thief.

Have you noticed that the less capable one always has to have preferential treatment and the logic applied is one way to the advantage of the less capable? This is preferential treatment which is what the less capable need as they cannot compete under fair play and if they don't get their preferential treatment they see it as not fair. Why is having an unfair advantage over others seen as fair? This is so because those who are less capable cannot compete or win without an unfair advantage.

One thing the less capable have difficulty in faking when they try to invert the truth or try to make others feel as if they should have less so the less capable one can have more is that they can only fake the obvious factors, but in life there are many other factors which play a part and aren't so obvious. These other factors would naturally adjust with capability so if someone was more capable these factors would adjust correspondingly, but someone exercising false one-upmanship won't be able to fake all these factors to cover up what he is faking and so they will show somewhere in the inconsistency of performance by the less capable. All less capable individuals who come out higher than they deserve are cheats, and all cheats are less capable.

However using the truth and exercising fair play against the logic of inferiority isn't unfair as it is not two ganging up on one, although the logic of inferiority will claim it is unfair – because it doesn't like the truth.

xiv. Don't Justify Yourself To Someone Who Is Stubborn

People who are stubborn don't like to honour anything above their mentality or understanding and have ridiculed me many times when I have come up with ways of solving problems beyond their understanding. If they cannot see it then it must not be possible, and if you argue with them you must justify yourself and if they cannot understand it they won't accept it and treat you as wrong. They try to treat others as guilty until proven innocent and quit often their victim will never be accepted as innocent and therefore never believed.

xv. If The Stubborn Don't Recognise It Then It Cannot Be

This is a bit like travelling on a coach with someone else and you see the Eurostar train shooting past and comment. By the time the other passenger looks around it has gone and there is no sight of it. So because you saw it and the other passenger didn't, you may experience the situation where you will be treated in the wrong because they didn't see it. Either they are reluctant to believe you (implying you are a liar) or they are too narrow-minded to accept it went so fast and they were too late to look around and see it. Just because they didn't see it doesn't mean it didn't exist. So just because they cannot understand something doesn't mean it is wrong.

For someone to correct me they must understand what I am getting at and pinpoint where I am wrong – otherwise I won't accept it as it is more a measure of reluctance to accept my way of thinking. I am definitely not going to accept their way of thinking where they make small look bigger than big, invert the truth and use two wrongs to make a right as well as hold strengths to ransom by being the weakest links in the chain. I am not going to be held to ransom by their inabilities and limitations.

If someone who is stubborn tries to bring me down to below their level trying to exercise authority on me and expecting me to justify myself to them – I won't.

xvi. Key People

Sometimes Key People within society are what they are knows as – literally. Some of them in positions of authority act like keys to progress for others and only if your face fits theirs will they unlock the next door for you to progress in life. If they don't like you they will hold your progress to ransom because they are the key to your freedom.

xvii. Popularity Is Linked To Privileges, Inferiority & Wrongdoing

People who don't stand out are more popular than those who do; but also privileged people (whether they stand out or not) often have more chances of popularity through buying power.

Someone who is privileged and/or thick will get more support than what is fair; whereas someone who is disadvantaged and/or gifted will be treated worse.

Let us examine the two situations. The thicko needs support and gets some but if privileged will get much more; the gifted will be ignored and rejected through jealousy and if disadvantaged won't get any opportunity so be left to rot.

This is exactly what happened to me around the millennium with New Labour's promise of fair deals and chances. Overpaid thickos who were underqualified and favoured over others were offered more financial support off the state when they had already been given plenty and were in no need of extra support; whereas disadvantaged gifted individuals who had circumstances against them through no fault of their own and had been discriminated against were not offered any financial support because they were overqualified in spite of being in financial poverty and in more need of support to get out of the trap of being underpaid. So this shows the privileged rot supporting privileged rot over genuinely disadvantaged gifted individuals. Why? Because the genuinely gifted are a threat to these sick and twisted individuals in high places trying to control society.

Once the privileged rot is in control the will decide what is right and wrong and wont honour the truth. They need to tailor everything in their favour to maintain their corrupt false-one-upmanship mentality and ways but they will never be genuine or change the truth that they are false. They fear better, more capable individuals outdoing them so have to do everything they can to suppress our progress.

Sorry, but there is no incentive to try constructively where effort is returned with persecution, punishment and yet more attempts of discrediting while the cheats, liars, backstabbers and corrupt do all they can to come out on top even though they are not worthy of it. I would not get anywhere under normal channels so I have used my imagination and the disruptive side of me to progress, so at least I will succeed in a rather destructive way – by using the truth

I would be happy to be seen at the bottom of the class by the privileged rot – at least I am innocent and not false, whereas some of the rot is guilty and corrupt. When treated properly I can rise to the top and possibly above the rot; but with society being so corrupt for many years I have been at the bottom.

There is too much support for the greedy and too little support for the needy. This is why there are so many delinquents and dropouts within society – because their needs haven't been met and so it is not worth trying. They are punished more for trying. Run down estates and many people on long-term benefits are victims of the privileged rot in positions of authority failing them in their years of development and having too much control over their lives. I might have ended up like this but I managed to break free from the stranglehold of the privileged rot who were out to ruin my life. That is why I am doing this book to expose what they are trying to do to so many of us.

xviii. The Real Criminals

As I was nearly driven to becoming a criminal if all avenues of effort resulted in persecution and being treated worse than most, I have reasons to believe that there are many so-called criminals within society who are victims of abuse and neglect who didn't get the support they should have got and weren't able to fight their way forward or fight for their rights.

With so many victims labelled as criminals, this gives me grounds to believe that the real criminals – especially the ones behind making victims of neglect into criminals are people in positions of trust and hold authority over many. They abuse their positions and possible try to focus on other criminals so that their criminal ways aren't noticed. This is where they must be seen as innocent until proven guilty while their victims they have labelled and abused as criminals get treated as guilty until proven innocent.

So being someone in position of trust and having authority over others is not a guarantee that this person is trustworthy or has integrity. It is possible that if they have inferiority problems they will abuse the vulnerable to have a feeling of self-worth as they stand no chance in the real world.

Many in positions of trust and authority abuse these positions to undermine the strengths surrounding the truth of their victims.

Power in the hands of the less capable breeds evil.

xix. Being Seen In The Wrong Because Of Others Wrongdoing

Have you ever done something innocently and been in the right only to find you are seen in the wrong because of someone else's wrongful actions?

Take the situation where you are approaching a four-way roundabout (North South East West) from the south heading north with someone from the north wanting to head south. But someone from the east wants to head west or north and therefore has to go across the roundabout passed you.

You see the driver from the north going straight ahead (south) which means the driver from the east should wait and you head straight on too, but this driver doesn't wait. Instead he pulls out in front of the driver from the north and sees you pulling out in front of him only to find him hooting at you and accusing you of pulling out in front of him.

He is accusing you of doing what he did, so why is it okay for him to do it to another motorist, but not for someone to do it to him, and if he had obeyed the Highway Code he should have waited which means you would have entering the roundabout safely.

So he is in the wrong and you are innocent as he caused all the problems and is trying to make you look in the wrong.

This is typical of many things in life where you will be seen in the wrong because another person didn't do what they should. If he had gone into me on the roundabout, he would have caused it for pulling out too soon but I probably would have been in trouble for pulling out in front of him too soon even though if he had obeyed the Highway Code and waited I would have been in the right to have entered the roundabout when I did.

Look at every situation you are in carefully and when you get blamed for something try to see if the person blaming you is to blame for it. Quite often it can be.

xx. False Versus Genuine

When it comes to quality or genuine capability, the most capable within society are not ten times more capable than the least capable in general but just a bit more. Going by IQs someone of normal intelligence will have an IQ of 100 whereas someone of gifted level could have an IQ of about 150 – this is only 1.5 times the capability so capabilities are very near – a bit like heights of humans being compared – very few people are more than twice the height of the smallest. Genuine capabilities are not hugely different from the best to the worst. These are genuine powers.

When it comes to quantity or influence, there are some people with millions of times more resources – let us take a billionaire – this person will have millions of times more quantity than many of us but his capability might be below ours. So he can have a great influence through quantity or gravity. These are oppressive powers.

Genuine powers are not significantly more than others; whereas oppressive powers can be overwhelming. People who use oppressive powers do so because they don't like people with natural capabilities or powers of this and feel the need to use their powers to appear better. Many of these abusers will try to force their preferences into the lives of the ones with genuine powers of quality in order to hinder them so they can take control of society. It's a bit like how cowards on The Weakest Link use the power of the vote to vote the strongest as the weakest so they have a better change – the capability of the strongest link is a quality and is internal; whereas the power of the vote within the cowards is a form of gang power, a quantity and gravity and is not genuine. Those who use oppressive powers invert the truth and make small look bigger than big – just like how it has made all these cowards look stronger and the strongest look weakest.

So oppressive powers are what many people who are obsessed with huge resources use to take control of society and undermine those of us who are too good. These are what were used to deny me support for my illness and undermine my intelligence – and all responsible for this were in power who abused their gravity and authority to invert the truth and make me look in the wrong and at fault. There is no doubt about this since my care needs and intelligence were both recognised but used to the detriment of my wellbeing and where they shouldn't have been used. So my intelligence was used to undermine my care needs because I was too capable; whereas my illness was used to undermine my intelligence because I was too incapable. So you can see how those in power have changed the goal posts to the detriment of my wellbeing and contradicted themselves in what they have done.

Most success in life today which is out of proportion is not to do with capability as this type of success can only be proportional; so with it being out of proportion it must be where oppressive powers are used.

Oppressive powers are used by individuals who are spoon-fed, cradles and carried by institutions to abuse others in order to come out on top. Many people in high places have disproportionate control over society and it doesn't have to be a multimillionaire – it could be your boss. If he was just 50% more wealthy as a result of better opportunities and pay as well as his rank ad you were much more capable than him, He would still have more weight as his gravities over yours (quantities/external influences/false values) are disproportionately more than your capabilities (qualities/genuine capability/strengths) over his, and he must be seen by his weight (mass times gravity) rather than his true capability, so this is where they need to bring external factors in so that they come out on top and appear better. They don't like being compared by capabilities because they are less capable.

Similarly we come across many other factors linked to inferiority as substitutes to make them look better. Speeding and overtaking is one such thing by the less capable as this helps make them feel better, but speed is not a quality but a quantity and is linked to a need to cover up inferiority than being a good driver. You don't need to be faster to be better – and similarly you don't need to be on top to be the best. Similarly status, wealth, power, authority and control are not qualities but quantities for the less capable to use.

A ponce is defined as “an effeminate person or an individual who attempts to fake having intelligence, class or culture”. The term originated in the UK and came to prominence in the 1960's. Wearing a false image is a form of make-up, so both descriptions can be used to describe those who exercise false one-upmanship. Ponces try to progress by using disadvantaged individuals as stepping stones as well as hiding their faults behind the circumstances of the disadvantaged. They try to look glossy on the outside but hide their bad side underneath.

Everyone who demonstrates false one-upmanship is inferior and has the following characteristic:

- An inflated ego;
- Diluted strengths by trying to make their genuine capabilities cover a greater volume so their strengths become diluted or thin;
- Puffed up like a sponge where there are many gaps in their strengths.

xxi. Double Inferiority

All charlatans who abuse others to progress are corrupt and cannot win without cheating, wrongdoing or abusing. Therefore, all charlatans have double inferiority.

Charlatans are less capable generally than they can accept; they lack moral standards, integrity, trust etc. so as well as having inferiority of the inner-self they display inferiority in their standards of behaviour towards others.

- Every act of wrongdoing is an infliction of inferiority
- Everyone who is pretentious inflicts inferiority on others
- Everyone who tries to exercise false one-upmanship is a charlatan
- Charlatans try to make false one-upmanship look genuine and suppress the progress of natural potential of others who have extra

talents

xxii. Assuming The Worst Of You

If someone is assuming the worst of you and this is nothing like your true character, then the chances are that this person cannot compete with you and wants to compare your worst with their best.

People who cannot compete cannot win in a fair way or comparing like with like, so they look for ways to look better which aren't logical or factual. They cannot compare like with like i.e. their best with your best because they are insufficient; but they may be able to run you down and compare their best with your worst.

There is no truth in this comparison when it comes to facts or like with like and there is a detailed explanation of this later on in this section under "Four Better or Four Worse".

Those who cannot compete properly also don't like the truth as it really hurts and cannot be changed. Lies can be made up, tailored and changed as required; but the truth is set in stone and cannot be changed.

xxiii. Nothing Is Better Than The Truth

The truth is one hundred per cent correct and nothing can beat it. Lies are incorrect and therefore relatively inferior to the truth; whereas assumptions and beliefs can only be as good as the truth if they are 100 per cent correct. However, most beliefs and assumptions carry some element of fault and therefore are relatively inferior to the truth.

Sometimes however, the narrow-minded who cannot think beyond the obvious can be so sure of what they are thinking they see their beliefs and assumptions as 100 per cent correct and wont honour the real truth because they are blinkered. Such people will try to force their choice over the truth onto someone else and this is infliction of inferiority where the truth has been inverted to look wrong so that what is wrong looks right.

Opportunist wrongdoers often rely on two wrongs making them look right and they behave as if everything they do is right. No number of wrongs can make a right.

xxiv. Cocky Colleague

Before satnavs became popular I went with a senior colleague on business and he used his Psion satnav to get directions but I didn't need a satnav – I knew my way about. While he was driving he was showing off with his satnav; but when it was my turn to drive he wouldn't let me use my knowledge but insisted we used his satnav to give me the directions which way to go. He liked to exercise false one-upmanship but needed spoon-feeding to do so (with his satnav) but didn't like to see me outperforming him with my knowledge of getting around the roads so he made me look as if I needed spoon-feeding like he did.

Later on we were discussing theories and something was new to me. My imagination got going and I came up with a suggestion which wasn't directly conclusive from the information given. He spoke down to me telling me that I couldn't conclude that from the information given and told me I was talking nonsense even though I was on the right track; but then he probably needed to be spoon-fed with this idea as he has no idea of it coming to mind naturally. He obviously doesn't realise that some of us have imagination and problem solving minds which this way I would have gone along without being told. It seems like he didn't like to see me doing it naturally and so belittled me yet further.

On another occasion he didn't respect my understanding or intelligence and so I didn't honour his authority. He got a bit cocky with me telling me that as he is above me he must be more intelligent; so I started telling him what to do. I said that if that is the case then as I am more intelligent than he is I am senior to him and he should do what I say. He got annoyed that I wouldn't respect his authority, so I told him that I wouldn't respect his authority if he didn't respect my intelligence. If he thinks a higher position means more intelligent then I will claim that higher intelligence should mean a higher position.

As a result, I couldn't get on with him and so sank to the bottom of the team with everyone else doing better. I wasn't going to try when it resulted in punishment and being belittled.

I have always been bottom of the class since others started inflicting their inferiorities on me as I see coming out on top for those unable to compete fairly and therefore obsessed with coming out on top through cheating and/or abuse. I have always been put down for trying to progress when less capable individuals have tried to come out on top, so it isn't worth trying where others are concerned and so I go about doing things on my own and because I am on my own nobody can get one up on me.

After all, the rot always comes out on top; so does inferiority as it gets there by destroying others who are better. Those at the top are rarely the best but nothing more than smaller individuals standing on higher platforms (privileged or cheating) trying to look bigger when they are really smaller.

xxv. Trying To Win On Doubt

Here is something where someone with little or no knowledge tried to make out he was better than others. It was all based around chances of confidence and doubt. This is a true experience but I have adjusted the incident to make it into an ideal example of idiots coming out on top (or trying to).

I went into a pub and saw someone I had met before who isn't too knowledgeable. It turns out there was a pub quiz on and he wanted to join up with me as a team. I wasn't particularly bothered in how well we were likely to do as it was a bit of fun; but he seemed to want to prove himself under false pretences.

As the questions were asked he waited for me to come up with an answer before he gave any suggestions. I noticed that if I was confident he would agree with me; but if I was in doubt he would disagree with me. Whenever he disagreed with me he didn't come up with an alternative. If it was balanced and either way he would make a guess and try to look as though he knew better.

After the first half, I analysed his replies and noticed what had been going on with his answers and choices, so I decided to play the fool and was over confident when I had no idea, but doubtful when I knew the answer. Acting this was tricky since it wasn't natural but I managed to distort my certainties of how sure I was.

When the quiz was answered, all the answers I was sure of in the first half were correct and as he had chosen these answers he was correct as well; but some of them in doubt were correct while more were incorrect. So the ones which I was confident in we both got correct; but with more of the doubtful ones being incorrect and these are the ones he disagreed with me then as far as he was concerned that meant he was correct for disagreeing with me, and so he claimed to have scored more than me in the first half – and didn't even answer a single question.

So when the second half was answered, he was in for a shock. About half of the ones I acted sure of were correct while the other half were incorrect so he only scored on the correct ones; but all the ones I was significantly in doubt over were correct and he scored nothing here for disagreeing with me. My score in this second half outweighed his by far and the look on his face was disapproving.

Combining the two halves my score was significantly more than his, but luck could have been his way if I hadn't realised his tactics and going by the way he allocated points to his scoring method he could have scored more than me without answering a single question – like he did in the first half. His way of scoring is not for not giving a correct answer (which he would have scored zero as he didn't answer a single question) but based on whether he is correct when he agrees or disagrees with me.

At least I made sure that he didn't score more overall points than me on this occasion. He tried to be clever about scoring more than me in the first half but wouldn't honour that I scored significantly more than him in the second half. He never teamed up with me in a pub quiz ever again.

This shows how rot can come out on top.

This also shows how so many pretend they have an idea of something when they are playing on doubt. Supposing there was a murder case which had been going on for years, someone might say that they don't think it will ever get solved – yet they don't have any idea of what is going on with the detective work – they are preying on chances that it won't happen, not knowledge.

xxvi. Extreme Wealth Is Either Luck Or More Likely Engineered

We come across many people who become billionaires with handling money. Does that make them any better? If I were to play Lotto and someone else who did was to get six numbers would they be a better player? No. they are just lucky to have chosen the right numbers. Similarly with many highly wealthy people they were in the right place at the right time. But was it luck or was it that their face fitted the clique which controls enormous amounts of wealth and privileges who decide to grant huge amounts of resources to a handful of people whose faces fit?

It is more likely to be the latter as the chances of someone being in the right place at the right time on this scale is so small; and if it was achieved by chance then why aren't here so many more individuals with great potential and less money making it? It appears there are a handful of control freaks holding onto about 95% of the wealth of the planet who let it go to certain, selected individuals to look good. Do they do this to keep poverty in the Third World, unrest within ordinary civilised societies and wreck the development of many who could do a lot more? Why does wealth want to suppress the progress of their progress? Because it is linked to inferiority which is the root of all evil with money the fuel behind it.

If money wasn't so powerful then we could eradicate poverty across the globe, but doing this will take away the power form the rich and when it comes to genuine capability many of the wealthy aren't that capable because they rely on external resources (status, wealth, privileges, etc.) to be their driving forces and not their natural potential since for many their natural potential is nothing more than average and they wouldn't stand out in the crowd with that alone.

xxvii. Privileges Create False One-Upmanship

The privileged are mostly a breed of cheats as they aren't the best in general. Even if they were better their ranking would be tainted because they have had preferential treatment over others, so they should never genuinely be recognised as the best because the genuine factor of their success is "tainted". It is the gravity of the wealth and support they get which puts them on a higher platform and they perform better – or do they? Take this away – would they be where they are without it? They are only likely to be where they are because of a head start or being carried there. Is 200 miles in a car more capable than 30 miles walking? The wealthy can compare distances (200 miles versus 30 miles) but walking 30 miles is much more of an achievement than driving 200 miles.

So similarly many who are privileged aren't really achieving as much as the disadvantaged who achieve everything on their own. Standing on the ground gives you your real height; standing on a higher platform makes you look bigger than most when you could be smaller than average.

I could understand some maths worthy of A-level standard in junior school without any private tuition, mentoring or even any extra books – my ideas came out of my mind, and so as I was on my own I didn't get properly recognised, only what I was tested in schools which was within normal intelligence – yet there doesn't appear to be any news that Carol Vorderman had this potential in primary school.

She is recognised because she is better than normal and was given recognition and opportunity – but those who are recognised are often not the best because the best are often targeted by oppressive powers while those who are recognised are given unfair advantage over the majority of us. The best that have a disadvantage in another area are often targeted with intensity because the disadvantage can be used to ruin such people – just like the epilepsy was used to undermine me – because I was too good.

Both Sir Isaac Newton and Albert Einstein had older relatives who were specialists in mathematics and so they were mentored and supported – I didn't get any help and showed my potential, so if we were on a level playing field and I had the chance to develop I may have been better than them. It is not a certainty but I have shown my mathematical thinking is natural and more genuine than most, not been nurtured in me by privileges or mentors.

Therefore many of the privileged are just a load of cheats standing on higher platforms where oppressive powers work in the interests of those trying to come out on top rather than the best. That is how the privileged achieve so much domination and exercise so much false one-upmanship as they aren't genuine and don't achieve their goals in a fair way. They also operate in cliques as they have to be scheming against stronger people – like cowards on The Weakest Link.

Some of the privileged progress positively and don't exercise false one-upmanship which is okay and I am not having a go at them; but those who abuse their status and wealth to undermine disadvantaged individuals are the cheats I am trying to expose. If the privileged could progress without taking from or undermining the poor then the poor wouldn't have to go without for their gains; but since the distribution of opportunity is in the favour of the privileged, many gain at the expense of the disadvantaged and I cannot accept their success as being genuine.

The disadvantaged are standing on lower platforms while the privileged are on higher platforms, so the privileged don't have to achieve as much as the disadvantaged to look better. I am proof of this as I am one who comes into the disadvantaged group and managed to show myself as better than some of the privileged, even though some still try to belittle me. At least I am genuine, not false.

xxviii. The Stockholm Syndrome

The Stockholm Syndrome is simply the denial of factual solutions by people for varied reasons, unable to clearly see, as a result of relentless brainwashing and a purposeful mind control.

Derived from the 1973 hostage incident in Stockholm, Sweden when victims after six days of captivity in a bank, resisted rescue attempts and later refusing to testify against captors, the name has been associated with kidnap victims under extreme emotional stress/duress.

Fear becomes the determining factor, and a means of a survival in a hostile environment. Applicable to battered-women, prisoners of war, the Stockholm Syndrome is widespread amongst the average populace, as well, in these times of catastrophe and worldwide wars.

Unfortunately, sufferers of the Syndrome do not recognise this denial within themselves, continuing to be influenced by slave-masters and by others suffering from this Syndrome.

Could those servants who are puppets for the ones in control of others' lives have suffered in some way and now be suffering from Stockholm Syndrome without realising it?

xxix. Mistake Or Wrongdoing

A mistake is an isolated incident where something isn't done properly and we all make mistakes. Mistakes aren't that frequent in real terms and so shouldn't happen too often. So if a genuine mistake happens it will happen by chance. However if another mistake connected with the first mistake happens shortly after then the chance of two mistakes happening together is even less likely. Think of the Lotto – the first number is one in forty nine and all six is one in about thirteen million. So it is unlikely to happen. Similarly a chain of about six mistakes happening together is unlikely to happen (something like one in millions), so the only way it can be guaranteed to happen often enough for the cheats within society to gain is for all mistakes to be connected to inferiority of the inner-self. Inferiority of the inner-self affects many factors and you will see some people not just making an isolated mistake but many connected. Take for example a driver – we all slightly speed and may make a few errors from time to time, but these are often isolated. However, if you see a driver who is excessively speeding, undertaking, cutting others up, dangerous manoeuvring, going through red lights and more, these are not genuine mistakes but acts of blatant wrongdoing associated with inferiority of the inner-self.

I can normally tell the difference between genuine mistakes, handicaps and evils of inferiority. Evils of inferiority are often used by the obsessed that use whatever power they have at their disposal to adopt a win-at-all-costs policy against someone else. They are always competing to look better, but like I have already said coming out on top isn't proof of being better; but it is a must for the less capable to feel better.

Many mistakes made by government departments to cover up wrongdoings, impropriety, denial of rights, defamation of character, abuse, betrayal, neglect, etc. are not human errors but wilful acts associated with the evils of inferiority.

XXX. Forgetful Or Intrusive

How often have you told someone something and find they ask you something again or claim you said something else? This is an ideal way for someone to cross-examine you or intrude into your privacy.

When you answer a question you are providing information from several variables to arrive at the answer, but if the same question is asked from another angle you might end up answering it with other factors. The more factors they have the wider the knowledge beyond what they were asking in the first place.

Also, some may think you are trying to keep something away from them and will try to misinterpret it in their favour so that there is a discrepancy and they will try to get you to justify why you said something and changed your mind when it was their deliberate different interpretations they made in order to quiz you.

If anyone tries to tell you that you said something else, they are going by interpretations on their side and in situations where you suspect there is jumping to conclusions so that you are made look as if you said something else or changed your story, the best thing is to stay quiet and not answer.

The best way to make this obvious is to have a printed message which you can hand someone when they start so that it is not seen as a knee-jerk reaction to being caught out. Something like:

> "Too many misunderstandings, too much jumping to conclusions and too many different angles of attack where I have to justify my innocence is being used to intrude into my privacy. It is not up to me to prove my innocence; it is up to you to prove me guilty. I am innocent until proven guilty and therefore not answering anything as a result of being treated guilty until proven innocent. Answering specific questions will enable you to intrude so I am not answering anything; and as this has been prepared up-front, it bears nothing to what you have just said to me.

xxxi. Coming Out On Top Is For Cheats

Coming out on top is a must for the false, obsessed and weak because this can be accomplished but they cannot perform as the best; whereas those who are the best are happy with the fact that they are better than most. Qualities such as talents, capabilities, etc. are internal and what make some come out on top, but quantities like status, wealth, privileges, etc. are external and not a reflection of one's potential are so often used to come out on top. This is where false one-upmanship is used a lot; and to maintain it there will be a lot of wrongdoing committed as such cheats cannot stay on top without wrongdoing.

Many wealthy people's wealth is nothing more than ill-gotten gains through perverted tactics and undercover scheming.

The genuine don't compare themselves individually with others but see themselves where they are in society (something like in the top few per cent) rather than by individual so don't need to try to come out on top and if things aren't good enough they will gladly respond in accordance with how they are treated – if they aren't recognised properly they will waste their talents like I did and I was happy to be seen as bottom of the class because it was a reflection of how I have been treated, not of my natural potential which is way above what most of them have. If someone gets the better of me that is only one person out of the population; I am still in the top few per cent. This will be explained under The Population Scale further on.

You can put a pint into a litre jug (waste talent) but you cannot put a litre into a pint jug (false one-upmanship). I don't care being seen by small contents (quantity) as I have shown myself to be more of a litre jug (quality = litre); whereas the cheats are filled to the top (more quantity) have shown to have qualities more in line with a pint jug. So they are like overfilled pint jugs which cannot hold more than a pint; whereas I am an undefiled litre jug which hasn't had even half a pint put in me; but as a litre jug, I still have greater capacity than the pint jugs even if they have more put in them. Even if a gallon was put into one of them it would still not be able to hold more than a pint so all the excess resources or quantities put into the pint jug will go to waste – why not put more into a litre jug and stop wasting what pint jugs cannot hold?

Similarly, the bigger the area you spread a fixed volume of water over, the shallower it becomes; so the more some try to come across as knowledgeable, the more shallow their knowledge.

Cheats are unable to win purely on qualities; they have always had to bring quantities in order to win – which means they are cheats, liars, backstabbers and wrongdoers in order to win. I was prepared to become a criminal to get justice and if I became one without justice it would have been yet more proof that those who are labelled as criminals are victims; whereas the real criminals are squeaky clean with bureaucracy and being wrapped in cotton wool protection associated with their status and wealth (qualities not qualities). Quantity can never be a quality. Quality is a born instinct/gift which cannot be bought or artificially made. I am proud of what I am, not what I haven't achieved through normal channels (or what the Controlling Elite have subjected me to for their false one-upmanship) but what I have managed to overcome and achieve given the circumstances. I have proven my giftedness and have overcome plenty more than what many at the top would ever have coped with. Most at the top would be big cry-babies for the slightest of inconvenience and I don't think any of them would have the mentality to cope with all the oppression and persecution I experienced. Most people who experience a fraction of what I went through would have their lives ruined, so as well as having double special needs when I was younger I have double success which outshines what the majority of people at the top could demonstrate since their status and wealth is all down to quantity; whereas my achievements are all down to quality.

Maybe that is why they continue to act like cowards on The Weakest Link looking for every excuse and opportunity to undermine those of us who are stronger and make us look The Weakest Link when they are all weaker.

Quality is my strength; quantity is my weakness. Quality is their weakness; quantity is their strength. Quality is internal and a measure of one's strengths; quantity is external and not a true measure of one's strengths.

Before my problems I naturally rose to the top without trying – and that's what nature intended; but one abuse started coming in, those who won were always against people doing better and had something of an inferiority or chip on their shoulder they were trying to hide and so coming out on top was a must for their survival and to live a life of false one-upmanship to hide their inferiorities.

So people who slot into place at the top naturally are genuine; others who are aggressive and fight their way are abusers and cheats since they win through abuse and undermining stronger people.

xxxii. Opportunist Wrongdoers

All opportunist wrongdoers have to do wrong to achieve their goals or an element of satisfaction because they cannot do it by abiding to the rules (or the law) because of their lower capabilities. Coming out on top gives them a buzz, but people who are happy with their capabilities and don't have a desire to compete as someone overtaking doesn't matter and are happy not aim to be seen as on top as it is not important, and coming out on top doesn't mean being the best – this is only a must for those who are less capable because they try to come out on top (through wrongdoing) to make out they are better – in an attempt to hide their inferiority and the truth surrounding it. However, if someone who has done nothing wrong is a victim of an opportunist wrongdoer and consequently suffers an element of degrading or defamation of character such as being treated in the wrong for not doing what the wrongdoer wanted, the victim may not take this peacefully since it may be seen as taking what is rightfully theirs away such as pushing into a queue and retaliation may take place.

People who are less capable expect you to treat them better than they treat you; but if you were to treat them in the way they treated you it would be wrong.

Let us take for example speeding motorists. All motorists speed a little but it is mostly human error, so doing thirty two in a thirty zone wouldn't warrant being treated in the wrong; but some will do forty in a thirty zone knowing they can get away with it (opportunist wrongdoers) and this gives them success over the law-abiding motorists and they get a buzz out of it.

Some less capable motorists don't like law-abiding motorists who stick to the speed limit and especially so when they appear so much better. Such drivers with Small Person's Syndrome try to compete and outdo decent drivers which show the inferiority problems they have and not being prepared to accept the truth that they are less capable.

They wrongdo because it is a compulsion to make themselves look better than they really are and to hide their inferiority. They are persecuted by the inferiority of their inner-self, and because they are their own weakest link they will never be free from it and will carry it everywhere with them. Their victims are only temporary affected by the negativity of their inferiorities since victims have strengths and can work in parallel with the inferiorities of the wrongdoers, whereas the wrongdoers will always have their weaknesses in series with their strengths and be a prisoner of their inferiorities for life. We are all restricted by our limitations but many of us experience limitations enforced from outside; the less capable experience internal limitations because of their inferiority of the inner-self.

I have been treated as subnormal but that didn't stop me from progressing to way above what those who tried to restrict me. This labelling was used as an external limitation to stop me from progressing but I made it temporary and worked in parallel with it and so my strengths have taken me further. However, the ones responsible for undermining me will undoubtedly have inferiority of the inner-self for trying to hold me back.

In fact, it is easier for someone who is an opportunist wrongdoer and uses every opportunity of wrongdoing to progress to succeed corruptly than it is for a gifted person to be given equal opportunities and get what they deserve. This is why there is so much rot at the top where the unscrupulous let power and greed take over their lives and they lose their integrity. Look at football starts speeding over a hundred mph thinking they are a cut above the law and can get away with it; and MPs with their expenses scandal. This is an example of two acts of inferiority at or near the top. Their standards are worthy of spoilt overgrown children. There is more undercover wrongdoing by people in high positions than by people at normal level – like with privileges they can "buy" their way out and use backhanders to get preferential treatment to stay whiter than white.

xxxiii. Whiter Than White

People who appear spotless are often the biggest wrongdoers in life. We all experience some tainting as nobody is perfect, but some are blatant wrongdoers.

To have that bit of tainting through human error and normal activities is nothing to be ashamed of so that wouldn't require cleaning; however blatant wrongdoing is something not to be seen and so this is where the wealthier and control freaks "clean" themselves to look spotless – the trouble is when they do this they clean the natural tainting they have and so by appearing spotless it shows that it is not the natural tainting they have cleaned as they wouldn't go this far for this, so it must be blatant wrongdoing or opportunist wrongdoing they don't want to be seen as having committed.

Such people like to have polished paths for an easy ride in life – they haven't had to really achieve anything, so a spotless image is a reflection of being overprotected and covering up wrongdoings.

Quite often the victim won't be protected by law and the only way for the victim to get what is rightfully theirs is to deal with it themselves and in doing so end up as being seen as the criminal because the wrongdoer has more rights than the victim. If someone entered your property and wouldn't leave peacefully, so you used force and injured the intruder, you would probably be punished more for taking action to protect your belongings from the intruder than the intruder will get for entering your property without consent.

Don't trust anyone with a glossy image – it is like the rot at the top which has been wiped away but has still been committed.

xxxiv. A Chain Is Only As Strong As Its Weakest Link

Weakness, not strength has a control over others. Stronger people cannot strengthen weaker people, but weaker people can undermine stronger people. So this is where we can show that control freaks are not the strongest but the weakest of all those they control. A control freak doesn't maximise the efficiency and add strength to the team but mostly undermines those who are stronger and acts as the weakest link in their chains, thus everyone stronger than the control freak will experience undermining.

So control freaks don't control by strength; they control by weakness making their weakness the weakest link in others chains.

xxxv. Comparative Misunderstandings

There have been numerous incidents where the stubbornness of the inferior have tried to correct me who have been too blinkered to understand what I was getting at.

For example supposing a bar of chocolate Bar A cost 50p four years ago, then went up annually to 52p 54p 56p and now 58p; and the same was true for a different bar of chocolate Bar B. I could state, "The prices of Bar A and Bar B are the same as they were four years ago". Someone would take this to mean that I have stated that the prices of Bar A and Bar B haven't changed in four years; but I am not on about the actual prices, I am on about the comparative prices, which have remained the same for the past four years. There have been many other situations where I have been talking comparatively or relative to something else and not the full value where I have been treated in the wrong, and the other side fails to understand and accept my side which is logically correct. So if anyone sees me in the wrong for their inability I see them to be inflicting negativities associated with their relative inferiority on me holding the overall progress to their ransom as they are the weakest link in the chain and we all know a chain is only as strong as its weakest link.

xxxvi. Punish Where Possible

In life, your goodness is often taken for granted and you receive little or no recognition for it; whereas you do something incorrect or wrong you can almost guarantee you will get punished or undermined. Take for example driving – you could be a safe and courteous driver and make the smallest of mistakes and end up being punished more than many motorists who lack courtesy and safety on the road.

Like with insurance (and many other things like bank charges) if there is anything they can penalise you for they will be quick to; but if it is something you deserve they will try to avoid giving it to you.

Look at drinkers – the government wants to increase the price of alcohol to deter binge drinking – but that penalises the responsible drinkers.

xxxvii. Don't Be Exploited

Being exploited for your qualities without receiving the necessary respect, recognition and reward can result in you being punished more than others for being more productive and trying while the slackers get away with their slackening.

Consider the following situation where five members of a team all doing the same work in principle and contributing 20% to the production. However, one is particularly eager and enthusiastic and does 30% which if the others don't slacken would make production at 110%. But the others slacken and perform at 17.5% which is just over half of what the enthusiastic one is doing (17.5 compared with 30).

This goes on for a while with production at 100% and he gets no praise or thanks for his extra work and so decides that enough is enough and he is not going to do more than he is paid to do so immediately drop back to 20%. The slackers however take a time to realise this and continue slackening and therefore production slackens to 90%.

The boss at the top notices this drop and sees the enthusiastic one as the only one who has slackened and therefore treats him as the slacker while the real slackers continue to get recognised as better.

You can see the one who did the most and more than what he was being paid for ends up being punished for not maintaining this "extra, unpaid" level while the slackers get away with it.

This has stopped me from putting extra in while others slacken and get away with it. I am not going to be punished for trying and treated as slackening when the real slackers get away with it and are treated better than me.

xxxviii. Experience Or Opportunity

To progress in life you need opportunity, but you are also expected to have some experience as well. For experience you need opportunity; and for opportunity you need experience.

Experience can be gained, but capability cannot be; and this is one thing which the privileged who are likely to have more experience but less capability don't like.

They use "a lack of experience" as an excuse to undermine ones who have greater potential or who haven't had a fair deal in life, but how did they start? They once had no experience but it wasn't a barrier for them and didn't stop them from progressing, so why do they use "lack of experience" as an excuse to undermine the many that haven't had the chance to make the most of their potential? Because they are less capable and need preferential treatment and use double standards.

xxxix. The Wrong Tone Of Voice

The tone of voice others have used against me has been the biggest emotional abuse factor which has made me have a very strong and intimidating voice in return. They speak in the wrong tone upsetting me and consequently I reply in an appropriate tone worthy of how they spoke to me.

Even today, if people talk to me in the wrong tone of voice as if they have authority over me and tell me what to do, I might overreact. A nasty voice is one of the biggest forms of emotional abuse by those who abused me and I have developed a loud voice in defence at these. I have loudly answered people back in public or on trains and left them in tears for trying to talk down to me. I used to say to bullies in front of many, "I am not pulling my trousers down for you" which meant I was not going to let them take control of me. It doesn't sound very nice when others hear it and it can be very humiliating.

There have been many incidents where someone can upset me and I object to their way and they raise their voice because they didn't like how I objected to them and I then raise my voice back at them and they get upset at how I spoke to them. They tend to go on about how my voice upset them but have no consideration of how they upset me which made me raise my voice. Arguments break out trying to blame me but not honouring my side of argument.

Very often the other side tries to destroy my side of argument making it drag on. I let them have their say and honour their side immediately but they don't for me and keep interrupting so I have to go on and it takes longer. They then claim I am making an issue of it and having more of a say – they are making an issue of it by trying to prevent me having my say and because of all the interruptions it takes longer so I am not having more of a say like they claim. Their side of the argument is it is okay for them to object but not for me to. This causes another argument about unfairness and I defend my side with facts, fair play and truth whereas they need preferential treatment and invert the truth. They have to come out on top corruptly but if I win properly they won't honour it. They can only win through corruption.

If they can object to being upset at how they have been treated, then so can I, and if they try to supress my side where they have been nasty to me I will get nasty with them to have my say.

xl. The World Would Be Awful If Everyone Was Like You

I sometimes get told this, but I strongly dispute this because it is a manipulated view. I am only so destructive because of how I was treated by obsessive perverted individuals who were inferior and didn't have the potential to get the better of me. If everyone were like me, I would not have experienced any abuse and been able to deliver my best – far better than those who claim I am the cause of all the trouble. They are looking for trouble and trying to make others look at fault – but then this is the way those who are less capable can progress. They have to be negative to others who are better and try to do the see-saw act in order to progress – bring others down in order to rise above them.

In fact, if society was decent and fair, I could have done extremely well without any cheating or wrongdoing at all. That is not to say I wouldn't have made any mistakes since you don't have to be perfect to succeed but just be given a fair deal, whereas the less capable have to cheat, backstab, deceive and abuse to progress.

xli. Get Out Of My Way

When you are walking in a zone and someone comes from another zone into the zone you are in, heads straight for you expecting you to get out of the way, what should be done here?

Well, by continuing along your path you were already walking along you are likely to collide with the stubborn person expecting you to get out of their way. But you can logically prove them to be at fault since anything they hold against you then you can hold against them but one thing you have in innocence which they have in guilt is you were already walking along that way before they came into your zone, but they deliberately steered towards you. If they argue you walked into them, then so did they walk into you?

The fact is they caused it by purposely heading towards you and expecting you to get out of the way; even though you headed towards them and expected them to get out of your way as you shouldn't have to be forced to suffer for their gains and were there first. So, as you were already there first and didn't steer towards them – you are just sticking up for your rights not to be pushed about by others while they are trying to force you to suffer for their gains. So in principle, you are defending your rights while they are trying to steal your rights from you. They will try to make it look as if you are in the wrong but they caused it.

This also happens with motorists but to deliberately crash is a bit much. So motorists who try to force you over so that you do what they want and if you don't you will suffer are perverted. They are aggressive and impatient (both these are linked to inferiority) and very often drive too close to your rear. Such drivers are a pain in the arse and seem to enjoy getting up your backside by invading your private space with theirs since their private space in front of their vehicle intrudes into the rear of your vehicle – or in other words their private goes up your rear. After all that is what perverts get satisfaction in.

Too many motorists are impatient and make dangerous moves by undertaking, barging in, not waiting, etc. and many argue that they are in the right. If they were in the right then it would be right for all motorists to drive in that manner. If this were to happen there would be mayhem on the road, so what these drivers are saying is not that it is right to do this in the fair way which can be applied to all motorists; but it is right for them as a selected minority to do it as well as wrongdo where others should have to get out of their way and let them have priority so that others will be expected to suffer for their gains. What they are really trying to say is that they want preferential treatment – and this means they are inferior if they need preferential treatment.

With life in general, you will find that the inferior will always apply rules which can only be applied to a selected few – normally them and not everyone. The selected few have to have 'extra' and the remainder are expected to suffer. If there were two people and instead of sharing 50:50, one insisted 60 so the other had 40, it would be 60:40 but there would be more quality in the 40 than in the 60 even though the 60 was getting 1.5 times the reward, recognition and respect. Ones who gain at the expense of others are inferior.

The majority of Fat Cats are inferior as they take too much for what they deliver and expect others who do more than they are paid to go without.

xlii. You Are Never Wrong

Some people get angry with me and accuse me of never admitting to being wrong. Straight away they are incorrect because I do admit to being incorrect or having made a mistake when it happens, but I will not accept being treated in the wrong for not conforming to their preferences as if they have authority over me and have the right to treat me in the wrong if I don't do what they want. I am not going to let them hide their mistakes behind my mistakes or problems they have caused.

Because arguments break out they get remembered – they don't seem to remember when I admitted to making a mistake and it passed peacefully – it is when I argued against it because what they claimed wasn't true they remember it and claim I never admit to being wrong. Why should I give into them and admit I was wrong when I wasn't?

I do things in a different way to most and my reasoning has more factors than basic, so in general I am not wrong although like anyone I can make mistakes as I am human, but it is not mistakes which get thrown at me, it is accusations of not doing it correctly because I am doing it different to them, they don't understand or have sufficient information, or I don't honour their ways. They don't honour my ways so why should I be seen as wrong when they do exactly the same the other way round and aren't seen as wrong?

Well I have the freedom of choice to do what I want and so have they. They aren't honouring my way but I don't go round telling them they are wrong.

As long as there is mathematical or logical reasoning correct in what I come up with or it is factual, then I see myself as correct and what they want to do is their choice; but they try to force their preferences on me telling me what I should do. If I did to them what they did to me they would change the rules to tell me I was wrong in telling them what to do.

They seem to want to apply their beliefs as facts at me and if my beliefs are different to theirs I am wrong.

This is what I call "Factuation of beliefs" which is where the domineering, controlling side tried to force their preferences on the other side undermining their freedom of choice as if to tell them what to do. This is dictatorship and I will not tolerate anyone treating me in the wrong for doing things in a different way when what I am doing is perfectly correct and progressive with nothing factually, mathematically or logically incorrect/wrong.

If they refuse to let me treat them the way they treat me with the same rules applied which would make them be seen in the wrong from my perspective then they are too controlling, narrow-minded and unfair and I don't want to bother with them.

They treat me like this because they are less capable and cannot accept me for my ways. I might be incorrect with this belief and if so I would like to know why I get so much grief for being different and why tactics to invert the truth (making small look bigger than big) are used. These tactics are normally what the evil, less capable, selfish, greedy, etc. use who can only gain by making others suffer and my reasoning is consistent without any double standards or contradictions with small looking bigger than big anywhere.

I am entitled to do what I want and have my thoughts, so if others don't like them then tough.

xliii. Discrimination or Discrimination

There are two obvious types of discrimination: one which is where someone gets rejected because they aren't considered good enough for reasons which shouldn't be taken into account; and the other is where this is used as an excuse when someone is really considered too good and therefore gets suppressed.

I didn't experience genuine discrimination because if I did, I would have got support and there wouldn't have been all the restrictions imposed on me. So it is obvious I was treated the way I was because I was too good and because I had epilepsy it was a tool for discriminating against me and hiding their malicious attempts to subject me to years of oppression. There is no way I appeared backward so being treated like this was an abuse of power by control freaks in local government and government agencies in the South Wales areas of Mid and South Glamorgan.

It is not just wrongdoers in the public sector in South Wales but all over. If epilepsy was the reason not to get equal opportunities I would be getting much better opportunities now; but I still experience a level of discrimination by the pretentious as they look for excuses to devalue me. They can't use the epilepsy like others did years ago, but they can use the consequences of all this earlier discrimination which resulted in lack of experience to undermine me. Yet again it isn't genuine discrimination but all excises to undermine me so that the pretentious that need constant spoon-feeding to come out on top can get better opportunities.

This is very much like how cowards on The Weakest Link exploit the strongest where possible but when it comes to reward and fair play the strongest is treated like dirt and regarded as the weakest.

Most of those responsible for the oppression I experienced and the discrimination I experience today at the top are cheats, and all they have been able to teach me was how to suck poisonous eggs. They cannot get the better of me without preferential treatment, wrongdoing or abuse.

xliv. The Compensation Culture For The Corrupt

Compensation should be for real victims, not opportunist wrongdoers looking for opportunities to claim for being looked at in the wrong way or spoken to in the wrong tone of voice – well that's what seems to be the case with many who don't really suffer but get plenty; whereas many vulnerable victims who have been abused cannot get anything.

Therefore, compensation isn't seen as something in return for suffering but something to compensate the less capable for their inabilities so they seek compensation for the most minor of things. If they had to be inconvenienced in the slightest they would claim they were suffering and seek compensation. Well if they need compensation for so much, then so much is too hard for them and they aren't that capable. They wouldn't be able to cope with anything is what they are saying if they suffer when living a normal life (not being abused).

This shows that they must be less capable if they suffer more than most of us in life. They need to be wrapped in cotton wool don't they?

xlv. Cheats Don't Compare Like With Like

Cheats don't like to see others by their better side, but have a desire to see them by their worse side. This is because comparing the worst with their best gives them a feeling of being better – but they are only better than the worst of the others. Those who cannot compete also feel they have a right to cheat, or decide what is right and in effect they are acting as if they have authority over others (since people who abuse their authority tend to cheat and wrongdo while making out they are in the right). They treat others worse than they expect others to treat them and take rights and freedom away from others. If others treated them like this they would claim this is wrong – so why is it okay for them to do it? It is seen as okay because they need preferential treatment due to being less capable. They also progress by treading on others misfortunes (undermining victims who are stronger) and trying to prevent others progression.

So anyone who exercises authority on you which they haven't got is likely to be less capable since they are trying to have preferential treatment, be in control (to tailor things in their favour) and put you down.

xlvi. Knowledge Is Not A Measure Of Potential

Knowledge is not a gift, it is a privilege; and similarly potential is a gift, not a privilege.

Knowledge is like the contents in a jug; Potential is like the capacity of a jug. Therefore a small jug having more contents than a big jug doesn't mean the small jug has greater capacity; and similarly someone with more knowledge doesn't necessarily have more potential.

Potential and capacity are natural and what you are capable of holding; contents and knowledge are measures of support and opportunity or what has been given to you which are more directly connected with privilege power than natural potential.

Don't judge someone by how much they have been given; see them for what their full capacity is. An empty bucket should be more useful than a full jug as long as it doesn't leak – the only advantage the smaller jug has over the larger bucket is you know the full jug doesn't leak.

So this is the only risk you will need to take when something isn't filled to capacity or someone hasn't had much in the way of opportunity beforehand. You don't know if they can fulfil their potential or stay full to the top. If they cannot reach their full potential i.e. stay full due to a leak, you will know they have been damaged by some means.

xlvii. Speed Is Often Short-Cutting Not Efficiency

How often has someone been quicker than you at something, only to conclude at the most obvious answer and not taken all possibilities into account?

I have often noticed the narrow-minded trying to be quicker than me, but then I ask two questions:

- Are they too narrow-minded to see more of the picture; or
- Are they competing aggressively trying to make out they are more efficient (when actually they are exposing more of their weaknesses).

I don't like people trying to be better than they are as it shows too many faults and weaknesses which cannot be concealed completely. They say a job worth doing is worth doing well, so there are many reasons for superiority in a job not being rushed whereas there are many flaws when hurried.

The inferiorities include:

- Trying to be clever
- Showing narrow-mindedness
- Having an easy ride (not capable of a real challenge)

Think of some motorists – they like to go fast to show-off their vehicles and what they can do, because they cannot show natural potential of sufficient quality. It is like it in many walks of life where those who get to the top don't just rise to the top but compete in a corrupt way and shove others out of the way. Does that mean that all the rest who don't make it to the top are failures? No

It means that we all rise to our potential in our own way without competing to outdo others and that is where we drift towards.

I have drifted into the top 1% when it comes to intelligence even though I haven't made it half-way where competition comes in. none of those at the top where I work are anywhere near the top 1% so I may not be above them in rank but I am in intelligence.

So trying to be quick shows a possible cover-up for weakness. Don't rush, just do it at the proper pace and let yourself drift to your natural level without worrying about others.

xlviii. Too Much Speed Is Greed (And So Are Many Other Quantities)

Speed is a quantity which many like a lot of, just like status, wealth and other amounts. Wanting too much of anything is greed – and greed is often used to disguise inferiority. Such people want to overfill their pots or up to the brim – think of an ordinary person having an average-sized meal; a greedy one will try to put as much as they can on their plate – this is what inferior people do because they want to quantity-pinch at every opportunity (like penny-pinching). They are so desperate they do things which have very little gains such as a motorist overtaking in a dangerous situation only to arrive ten seconds earlier than if he had been patient and safe.

xlix. Laws Of Influence

Many of us are familiar with Newton's three laws of motion; well they can be adapted as follows:

- Everyone will progress at their natural rate unless acted upon by an external influence
- The change is character is directly proportional to the magnitude of the influence
- In the corrupt world, for every false result, there is an equal but opposite fact (small is made look bigger than big like cowards on The Weakest Link use the power of the vote and not the truth to make the strongest look the weakest)

I. The Population Scale

The population scale is something of a gauge of where you are within society or globally rather than directly compared on a one-to-one with someone else. It is easier for one person to cheat on someone else or be undermined so a one-to-one comparison with these cheating factors is not very accurate, so I prefer the population scale.

I don't need exact statistics or numbers but just logical reasoning to maintain my position where all the charlatans and cheats have absolutely no way of rising above me. Because it is based on fact and there is no distorting of the truth or hyping up of inferiorities it is so clear I honour this and feel free from the charlatans and perverted within society that I come across. I don't need to know my exact walking speed or the distance to London to know I wouldn't be able to walk to London in a day.

On a one-to-one basis or within a small community it is easy for a gang to get one up on you or to be discriminated against; or for them to get favouritism and preferential treatment. It is not possible for this to be done across the globe for one person though. You might get millions of small teams doing this but they are all individual cases and to get the better of one individual globally is impossible.

Think of two people A and B where A is brighter but B cheats and gets one up on A. The truth is completely inverted here on a one-to-one basis. When it is within a team it distorts the figures a bit with A swapping places with B.

Now think of this on the global scale. A is at a point and B is at another point both on the global scale. There is a gap of let's say one per cent of the population of the world when lined up in order of capability. Now one per cent of the world is an awful lot of people, so for A and B to swap sides one of two possibilities or a combination of both must happen:

Either A gets picked on individually by slightly more than one per cent of the population of the world and each one scores one point against A and rise by one person on the population scale but A falls by the cumulative effect of all this false one-upmanship on the population scale to below B's level.

Or B has to do the dirty on slightly more than one per cent of the population to make each of these individual victims fall by one person on the population scale but B rises by the cumulative effect of all this cheating on the population scale to above A's level.

So either way A has to be victimised by many or B has to cheat on many. There isn't enough time for one per cent of the population to pick on A or to be targeted by B so the gap between A and B would never be closed.

Let us take an example of people within society to get an idea of the scale. Someone has a community load of people against them but we will make this 50 thousand people for an example. Fifty thousand victimisations would take ten victimisations a day over five thousand days (thirteen years) to achieve. This is an awful lot of organising. So what is fifty thousand in relation to the world population?

Well in relation to 1 billion it is less than one per cent of a per cent, so being in the top few per cent when it comes to intelligence and all those who are charlatans being much lower down there is no way they can rise above me or bring me down to below their level by whatever means of gang power or colluding as the gap between me and them on the population scale is too big. With the gap being many per cent then those who would target me would have to be potential geniuses for the gap not to be too big, but since they aren't I am safe from their false one-upmanship.

Even 50 thousand compared with the 60 million population of the UK is below 1%, and I am in the top 1% in the UK, so with most charlatans being about normal they are out of reach. Therefore, even with the population scale of the UK I am safe. Even if I had to drop to the top 10% in the UK the gap is still too big for the charlatans within society to do the dirty on me this way because their intelligence is simply far too low down. This is no insult to people of average intelligence, but the charlatans are not normally gifted or particularly bright, so they are too far away to win.

The population scale of an office is not too much to close the gap as several could bring me down, so I don't look at small communities I look at nations and the global scale and they are what matter. Therefore on these scales I am safe from false one-upmanship by the charlatans irrespective of how many of them are obsessed with false one-upmanship and target me and others. There won't be enough upping of their position or downing of mine to close the gap sufficiently or swap sides.

Ii. Immediate Results

This is another fault charlatans and cheats have - they look at the short term gains on a small scale because it is in their interest; they are not interested in the long-term nor the overall effect within society - because they are selfish and impatient.

If it is possible for you to cheat it won't be worth the effort, if you are desperate to cheat you won't succeed because you are too far away. Sorry charlatans, as you are desperate this is one way you cannot win.

This is applicable to almost everyone - those who have a desire to get one up on you are too far apart to achieve the result. So you are safe. If they try to prove you wrong then they are desperate - just laugh at them and show no sympathy as they don't deserve any.

I don't bother competing since the more effort I put in the more persecution I get subjected to by the obsessed and those who are compulsive and less capable; so I wait for things to happen and come to me. If I don't get treated fairly then I shall continue to waste my skills and talents. It is not in my interest to try so I shall just be myself and if it upsets others then that is their problem. I am not infringing their rights, I am just not doing what they want; and if they try to stop me they are infringing my rights.

So I am myself and will always be above those who undermine me on the population scale because the gap between where they are and where I am on the population scale is too big for them to rise above me or bring me down to below them on this scale. So I am safe on this scale and that is where I see myself. I get on with life my way and don't compete with others – if things come my way then good, if they don't then others don't know what they are losing out in. I don't like competing since the cheats will always get preferential treatment and I cannot put the effort in when things are unfair – I won't bother trying. I am beyond recognition for what I have achieved in a different way as well as what I have taught myself and thought up for myself so I don't care if I am bottom of the class in the University of Life – I have something of a connection with genius which most people on the planet haven't.

Iii. Why Haven't I Bothered Trying

Well, it's not exactly true that I haven't bothered trying – I put a lot of effort in only to find that I was being punished for trying while the credits due to me went to the cheats, liars and backstabbers. Here is the final analogy simplified but based on a true experience to show how some people are punished for trying while slackers get away with it.

A team of five workers share the workload fairly doing twenty per cent each in order to achieve one hundred per cent. One of them is particularly enthusiastic and so does more and instead of doing his twenty per cent he does thirty per cent. His intention is to let the team perform at one hundred and ten per cent but slackers don't do their allocation of twenty per cent and so he ends up doing what they don't do.

Hoping for recognition he continues and the bosses at the top don't appreciate the extra he is doing so after weeks or months he begins to get fed up getting no recognition above the slackers. Therefore he decides to do no more than what he is paid to do and reduces his performance back to twenty per cent. However, the slackers don't bring themselves back up to their twenty per cent level but continue to slacken and as a result not one hundred per cent of the production is achieved.

The bosses at the top notice targets not being met but see no difference in the slackers; but noticed a big drop in the productivity of the enthusiastic one and so blame him for the reduction in productivity.

He performed way above what he was being paid for and then gets punished for not working at his best – even when he is not being paid for the extra he is doing; while the slackers underperform and get away with it.

This shows how punishment replaces recognition, reward and respect for the enthusiastic worker and so it simply isn't worth trying when you try, performing better than being taken for granted and punished if you don't do your best. So in these situations you progress in parallel where you are more likely to get the respect, reward and recognition you deserve.

This is exactly why I haven't continued bothering to try as I was taken for granted and when I refused to do more than I was paid for I got punished.

So I don't bother trying unless there is a guarantee of recognition, reward and respect for what I do. If this doesn't seem likely I won't bother as I am not going to sacrifice and put the effort in so that others reap the credits and rewards which should come to me.

A message for those who are out to win at all costs:

You are what you are and so there is no need to try to use a Red Hat to make out you are better than what you are since doing so to others who have greater potential means a battle between them wanting to fulfil their potential and you as an obsessed cheat who can only win by destroying the strengths of the better ones.

So trying to be better and winning is destructive and linked to evils of inferiority. Just be what you are and stop trying to bring others down since as individuals everyone is equal. Coming out on top and putting others down does not mean better but more likely to be an obsessed cheat or a small person standing on a higher platform trying to look bigger – and this suggests having a chip on your shoulder. This is the mentality which all sick and twisted individuals have, and there are too many of these who are nothing more than the rot at the top.

Better Times Ahead

30. To Finish With

So, to end my story, I have since rebuilt my life, doing reasonably well although it was a late start. I am now a structures engineer in the defence industry, a private maths tutor, a baritone taking part in various concerts as well as participating in choruses in various shows, and try to educate drivers to pass the Advanced Driving Test after having passed the test back in 2008.

My voice has certainly developed in more ways than one – probably in line with all the shouting and abuse of authority exercised on me when I was younger and so when treated inappropriately or spoken to in the wrong tone of voice I would raise my voice back and so it has had a lot of exercise. Some people have ended up in tears and walked out after I told them not to overstep their bounds and they are not in control of me when they have been too pushy with me. My voice is my best defence against being picked on as most people feel humiliated when I raise my voice. They say things which upset me but I don't get listened to when I am the victim, so I make sure I am listened to when it gets too much.

I also give talks on Science, Technology, Engineering and Maths as well as have credits for my speaking.

In spite of all these improvements and the shortage of maths teachers, I have made enquiries within local authority and academic institutions about doing more in maths and I don't hear anything from any of them. Maybe they are all false and small people standing on higher platforms who don't want someone like me. There is no need to discriminate against me like they do other than for reasons of discrimination like I experienced when I had epilepsy – the answer they would give is I have not got enough experience or what they mean as "snob value", but the truth is I am too good for them.

I also tour the UK as an incognito mystery shopper, evaluating shops, pubs, restaurants and more as I enjoy my leisure travels. I have certainly got a lot of credits which are genuine and not inherited through snobbery, wealth and privilege. One good thing when I go about incognito, nobody knows me and I am often perceived as someone of importance although I am dressed smart casual mostly. I have been thought of as a reporter, or even a down-to-earth millionaire. I am not the typical person but have something about me which makes people focus in on me.

I have received a lot more recognition over recent years with more positivity and appreciation generally and I feel that there is more respect for what I do. I have climbed a bigger ladder than I thought I would get the chance to do.

I am living proof that when treated properly someone can be very efficient and well-liked; but when treated badly by sick and twisted individuals with a chip on their shoulder in positions of trust and authority that don't listen to me or let me have my freedom and rights turned me into quite a nasty person. I can be very much a Jekyll and Hyde.

"You may see some truth on the outside; but there is always more truth deep inside which the cheats, liars, backstabbers and perverted try to hide."

31. Future Books

I plan on publishing other book when I can piece together some interesting pieces. They are likely to be published over the coming years, depending on time and content. The Small Things That Add Up is almost ready and likely to be published by later next year (2015).

Details will be detailed on www.j2r2r.com

i. Inferiority – The Root Of All Evil

I have started outlining a book on *Inferiority – The Root Of All Evil* as I have reasons to believe that inferiority is the cause of every problems within society (excluding those caused by genuine human error). It takes into account small being made look bigger than big, inversion of the truth and internal measures like mass being a quality and capability; and external influences like gravity being a quantity or scaling factor, and how one distorts where some get more support and others get too much hindrance. All the abuse and unfairness I experienced had an element of inferiority in them and there is no evil without inferiority. You can have evil without money but inferiority is always present in evil. Disability and handicap don't have evil within them; but evil has inferiority which gives it the negative direction combined with power which is often the dominant factor, and when combined these evil tactics take effect. ISBN 978-0-9926729-1-1

ii. The Small Things That Add Up

I also intend publishing some of the ideas in a book *The Small Things That Add Up* which helped me understand some maths worthy of A-level standard when I was in junior school. They aren't sophisticated but certainly exercise the mind. I have already prepared them as notes for my private tuition so intend getting them published. ISBN 978-0-9926729-2-8

iii. Strange Unexpectations

I am also looking at doing a book *Strange Unexpectations* on hundreds of incidents which have happened rather strangely. Things started to happen like this rather too frequently for a one-off and so I decided to record details down as well as keep proof where possible.

I don't smoke and had no reason to use a lighter until I decided to go camping. So one day for the first time in my life I bought a lighter at Tesco on my way home one evening to prepare for going away. I stopped to make a phone call by a hotel and five minutes after finishing my call and moving on it was reported that a fire broke out and the building was destroyed by the fire.

On another occasion I was going to go to London the following weekend, but on the Friday evening the week before this I felt that going a week earlier (the next day) would be better. So I went the following day and went around using the Underground. I got off at Kings Cross Station, went up the escalator. Several days later there was a fire on this escalator which claimed the lives of 31 people.

There are hundreds of uncanny experiences I intend putting together. ISBN 978-0-9926729-3-5

iv. The Funny & Beautiful Side Of The UK

The last area I am looking into writing is about my travels around the UK. *The Funny & Beautiful Side Of The UK* will incorporate details of various places for reasons worth mentioning but this will be a way off yet as I need to gather more information with my travels as well as mentioning some of the past, including some strange place names. I have included a few of the funnier ones but there will be beautiful ones also.

Six Mile Bottom is near Newmarket in Suffolk; Sluts Hole Lane is in Besthorpe in Norfolk; Swine is near Hull, Humberside; and Jingling Lane is in Kirkby Lonsdale, Cumbria

See pictures below. ISBN 978-0-9926729-4-2

40
SIX MILE
BOTTOM

SLUTS HOLE LANE

SWINE
Please drive carefully

Skipton
PUBLIC TOILETS
Jingling Lane

